Quiet Mind

Quiet Mind

One-Minute Retreats
from a Busy World

David Kundtz

Foreword by Steven Harrison

Conari Press

The lines from "Guardian Angel" are reprinted from *Twenty Poems of Rolf Jacobson,* translated by Robert Bly, Seventies Press, Madison, MN, 1976. Copyright © 1976 by Robert Bly. Reprinted with his permission.

Kabir's poem, "Breath," is reprinted from *The Kabir Book, Versions by Robert Bly,* Beacon Press, Boston, 1977. Copyright © 1977 by Robert Bly. Reprinted with his permission.

Cover and book design by Maxine Ressler
Cover photo © Jun Kishimoto/Photonica

ISBN-10: 1-57324-862-2
ISBN-13: 978-1-57324-862-4

Originally published in 2000 by Conari Press as *Everyday Serenity* under ISBN: 1-57324-162-8.

Printed in Canada
TCP
10 9 8

I dedicate this book of reflections
to all the clients, past and present, of my
counseling practice in gratitude
for your trust.

Your stories are for me,
without exception, pure grace.

+————————————+

*It is because artists do not practice, patrons
do not patronize, crowds do not assemble to
reverently worship the great work of Doing
Nothing, that the world has lost its philosophy....*
—G. K. Chesterton

Quiet Mind

Foreword

Author of *Doing Nothing*

We have collectively built an amazing world of technological wonder, of scientific marvels, and unparalleled productivity. But in this best of all possible worlds, we have learned so much about how to *do* that we have forgotten how to *be*.

We want to know what to do about this. We want to fix our lives. We want to build better lives. We want to do more. But, of course, *doing* can never bring us to *being*.

There is nothing to do.

In this realization something magical unfolds: Being is what remains when we stop trying so hard. In the stopping we discover the vast spaciousness of life, of love, of connection.

In *Quiet Mind*, David Kundtz leads us to those quiet moments of stopping and stillness in which we can just *be*. Thus he shows us that it is life that we are grappling with, not an abstraction, not a spiritual system to be learned and practiced, but the vital, ever-changing, often overwhelming, but always present life that each of us lives, every day, with no vacations.

Life is the unavoidable context with which we have been gifted, and that bestows on us the greatest of all opportunities, the discovery of the ground of being in each moment.

A New Way of Dealing with Life

Welcome

Welcome to a new way to cope with the demands of a too-busy life.

Welcome to a way that requires no difficult skills, adds no new burdens, and accommodates all spiritual systems and life-styles.

Welcome to all who want to do nothing—more often, more creatively, with joy, and without guilt.

Welcome to one-minute retreats that can be yours at any time of the day or night.

Welcome to a quiet mind—tranquility, calmness, and clarity—in the midst of a too-busy world.

Whatever you do

Whatever project you undertake, whether personal or business, spiritual or physical, noble or mundane, if you do not begin it from a mindful posture—from the quiet state of your being—you are headed for disappointment and failure. It's the nature of things. It's the *only* successful way to begin anything.

These reflections are based on, and are examples of, the practice of Stopping, which is doing nothing—for as briefly as a minute or for as long as a month—for the purpose of becoming more fully awake and remembering who you are.

You'll read about Stillpoints, the frequent, momentary pauses in your day. You'll also find examples of Stopovers and Grinding Halts, which are simply longer times of doing nothing but with the same purpose—becoming more awake and intentional, recalling what you want and need, where you've come from, where you're going, and how you'll get there.

Invitations

Here you will find brief invitations to take time for yourself, to rest, to find peace, to awaken, to remember, and to find ways to recognize what you may have forgotten, and how not to forget again.

Each of the reflections can serve as a Stillpoint—a pause for a purpose—to draw you to a moment of both rest and insight. You will also find meditations on longer times of rest and peace, and encouragement to fit them into your schedule.

Do nothing

These reflections are invitations to do nothing, and to "do" it with purpose, with meaning, and with value.

These reflections want to lead you to transform "wasted" time into the most important times of your life: times of stillness, solitude, peace, and equanimity.

Welcome to a quiet mind.

David Kundtz
Kensington, California

one

Still Moments
in Busy Days

Taking Time to See

Nobody sees a flower, really—it's so small—we haven't time, and to see takes time. . . .

—Georgia O'Keeffe

These are the days of the time famine," says Odette Pollar in her newspaper column aimed at helping people work smarter. She cites some interesting statistics. According to a Harris survey, the amount of leisure time enjoyed by the average American has shrunk 37 percent since 1973. In the same period, the average work week, including commute time, has jumped from fewer than 41 hours to nearly 47 hours, and in some cases up to 80 hours a week.

I like the term *time famine,* and starvation is certainly an appropriate analogy for our situation. Many of us are starved for time and we have a passionate desire to be fed. We are starving for those moments of solitude when we can just hang out, cleaning out a drawer or looking through old letters, with no pressure or guilt. Our starvation deprives us of the nutrition that those in-between times used to give us: a feeling of centeredness in our lives, of awareness of our spiritual needs and those of our families, a confident sense of self-knowledge.

Georgia O'Keeffe's words ring authentic as you look at her paintings of flowers. She spent many hours "doing nothing" with a flower. No time famine for her. Her artistic life in the desert was a statement against that idea. And we continue to benefit from the results.

In a famine—at least in the best of situations—those who have help those who have not. Thus a question presents itself: Where are you in the time famine, among the haves or the have-nots? Sometimes one, sometimes the other?

> *For have-nots: Today, stop and really look at a flower (or an O'Keeffe rendering of one). For haves: Help someone else to do the same.*

Rat Race

The metaphor of the rat race as a way to talk about the nature of contemporary life is instructive. I wonder about its origin. And just what is a rat race? I picture a maze in some scientific laboratory with a dozen rodents scrambling in all directions, trying with great frustration to find their way to freedom. Is that a rat race? Did anyone tell the rats they were in a race? Is there really a winner in a rat race?

And that we should choose this metaphor as a way to talk about the way we live our lives is . . . what? Alarming? "Well, we've got to get going and join the rat race." We do?

The metaphors we use not only reflect the way we live, but create the way we live. If we call life a rat race, it will tend to become one.

So let's change metaphors. Here are a few suggestions:

Life is a cat prowl. I envision slow and careful steps, a calm awareness of what is going on in my neighborhood, and a pace that suits my needs.

Life is a dog walk. I move now with lively interest, with stoppings and goings, encounters with other dogs, trees, and people, always ready to respond to a friendly petting.

Life is a fox trot. Here is a bouncy-stepped way to dance through life. Find a partner! You can always sit the next one out.

Life is a monkey march. Life is a pony canter. Life is a whale breach. Life is a swallow soar. Life is a pig parade. Life is an elephant lope. Life is a bear excursion (the one I'd pick).

Spend a quiet time today and pick your metaphor for life's journey.

Sounding Well

Rests always sound well.

—Arnold Schoenberg

Rests, as I understand them, are those moments in a piece of music when there is a passage of time but no sound. There is nothing. So Schoenberg, the composer, says that "nothing" always sounds well.

Hmm. Sounds like a trick, or a riddle. What's wrong with this statement? Buddhists might call Schoenberg's words a koan, a paradoxical riddle with no answer, used for discussion and teaching.

What can we make of it?

What gives life to the music is the feeling that jumps in during those pauses, during those sometimes incredibly quick split seconds when one note is just finishing its last echoing vibrations, but before the next one takes up the progression. The feeling slips, quick as a wink, into the gap and brings soul and life to the music. It is first felt, then expressed, by the composer. Then it is reborn with a familiarity, but also with the somehow new and unique contribution of each performer.

The feeling lives in the rests. And not just with the rests in music, but with the rests in bus driving and kindergarten teaching and homemaking and managing and selling advertising and cooking supper and picking up the kids and phoning customers and writing reports and on and on. The feeling lives in what you put into the rests. And the rests always sound well!

The quiet moments—rests—in your day make your whole day sound well.

As you go about your day today, notice the rests in the rhythm of the day.

Short Attention Spans

Modern life conditions us to skim the surface of experience, then quickly move on to something new.
—Stephan Rechschaffen, M.D.

Most of us spend our days staring at the huge Mountain of Too Much. Because most of us have too much of everything in our lives, it's easy to become overwhelmed.

One of the results of the Mountain of Too Much is that our attention spans get shorter and shorter, simply because there is less time for everything and we have to move quickly or be left behind. And our culture accommodates this pace.

The format of this book is an example of that accommodation: short sections, easily read in a brief time. So also are the ideas behind this book—ways for busy people with full lives to become spiritually awake and recollected, to relax, and to manage stress.

The challenge is balance. Do we have the ability to pay attention for only a short span of time? Or can we still call upon the often-needed skill of concentrating for long periods, with ongoing attention? Can we stay with a good process even though it is long or old or out of style?

Or are we compelled to "skim the surface of experience, then quickly move on to something new" just because it is new? For if we only skim the surface of life, we will, necessarily, become superficial.

Time spent doing nothing is an antidote to superficiality. It encourages and develops the skills to focus and pay attention for both the short and long hauls and helps us to probe below the surface, not just skim it.

Identify a project that requires ongoing attention and ask: What kind of quiet time do I need to support and encourage my ability to stick with it?

Every Day

One ought, every day at least, to hear a little song, read a good poem, see a fine picture, and, if it were possible, to speak a few reasonable words.

—Goethe

These are the things Goethe wanted in his day, every day. What do you want in yours?

Here is a snippet from a conversation I overheard in a busy downtown store between two middle-aged women:

"It's so good to see you. We just don't seem to get together as much any more, and it seems so many of us are saying the same thing. Why is that?" said one.

"I know exactly what you mean," said the other. "It seems that there's always just too much going on."

I'm convinced we all really do know what is happening to the way we are in the world, compared to the way we want to be. As the woman said, there's always just too much going on. The problem is not what we don't know; it's that we somehow feel powerless to change it.

When you have begun dealing with the problem of too much going on, you can start to identify just what you want to include in your "every day."

Even when you get together with your friend, you might discover that Goethe wasn't far off the mark. With your friend you might hear a little song (listen to some favorite music), read a good poem (discuss an article you recently read), see a fine picture (visit a museum or show a photo of your grandkids), or speak a few reasonable words (have an enjoyable conversation, catching up on each other's lives).

Today take some moments to decide what you want your "every day" to include. Repeat every day forever.

Going to the Post Office

In proportion as our inward life fails, we go constantly and desperately to the post office.

—Henry David Thoreau

You may depend on it," Thoreau continues, "that poor fellow who walks away with the greatest number of letters, proud of his extensive correspondence, has not heard from himself this long while."

I think I know the cause of our cultural, spiritual, and social problems today, just as Thoreau knew 150 years ago. Our inward life is failing.

Many of us know this, of course, and just knowing it doesn't change things. But what if someone—maybe you—could convince ten or twenty people to stop going to the post office for their information, and instead to stay quiet and recollected for a few minutes or even an hour a day to attend to their "inward lives"? What if I could do the same?

I used to think that what we needed was a saint or a prophet: a modern-day Francis of Assisi who would call us to our senses by the power of his example and love; or a Joan of Arc to inspire us with her disdain for the acceptable, her single-mindedness, and her devotion to her voices.

But we have saints; we've always had saints, canonized or not. We've always had prophets who are well attuned to their inward lives, who have voices of passion and love, voices of virtue and wisdom, who live lives of example and service, and who call us to the same.

And still many of us keep on stumbling to the post office.

Today, find a way to redirect your trip to the post office to a journey to your inward life.

Permission to Stop

The only way we could justify sitting motionless in an A-frame cabin in the north woods…was if we had just survived a really messy divorce.

—Ian Frazier

The author's words are a complaint that he had to have justification for doing nothing. He and his friends could not do nothing just because they wanted to; they had to have a very good reason, such as divorce. Then they could justify taking time off, or "wasting valuable time"—they had an excuse. They had just gone through something painful, and people would be hesitant to criticize them. Their guilt would be minimal.

But then he wisely throws out that kind of thinking and gives himself permission—no justification necessary—for doing nothing.

Unnecessary self-restrictions and false guilt burden many of us and keep us from the peaceful times we yearn for. Quiet time to be alone is not an optional nicety; nor is it just for the retired, the lazy, or those naturally inclined. It is for all of us. It is valuable time well spent.

And above all, it needs no justification other than its own noble purpose: to become more fully awake and to remember what you most need to remember about yourself and your life.

Do you need permission for doing nothing?
Here it is! Use it today.

Finally Getting It

Thanks for Nothing!
> —A young seminar participant

Often I find it difficult to get across the idea of doing nothing. I first discovered the resistance to the idea in myself. I continue to discover it in other people as I speak on Stopping.

We are just not used to doing nothing. It sounds and feels and seems wrong somehow. We want to fill up the time with something.

At a recent mini-seminar at a bookstore, a young man, about seventeen, entered late, wearing his hat backward and carrying a skateboard. He sat down in the middle of the front row and paid close attention to what I was saying.

Midway through the presentation he raised his hand and said, "What you're saying is that we should spend a lot of time just thinking about the really important things in life, right?"

"Nooo," I answered, "I'm suggesting that's something we should *not* do! Just do nothing, don't try to think about anything!" My answer was met with a vexed and quizzical look. The look remained, and as I continued the seminar his attention stayed focused on my answer to his question, and not on what I was saying.

After a little while, he stood up quite suddenly, smiled at me, gathered up his skateboard and backpack, and began to leave.

"So long," I said, interrupting my presentation. All eyes were on him as he took the opportunity to say, "So long! Oh, and thanks for Nothing. I appreciate it!"

I think he meant it.

Today, consider the question: What is my understanding of doing nothing?

Reality Check

It will never rain roses: When we want to have more roses we must plant more trees.

—George Eliot

Occasionally someone will say to me, "Just sitting and doing nothing seems to be running from the real world, hiding from what you don't want to face." My response is to reiterate that intentionally doing nothing is indeed the *opposite* of running and hiding. This is *because* it brings you face-to-face with—even to the point of embracing—the most important and challenging aspects of human life, those based on your meanings and values.

As Eliot says, if you want roses, plant trees. What doing nothing can do is help you *know* what you really want—is it roses, or gladiolas, or redwoods, or none of those?—so that you don't end up with a beautiful garden of what you don't want.

The English novelist quoted above, George Eliot, speaks these words from personal experience. Born Mary Anne Evans into the male-dominated Victorian world, she led her rich and complex life successfully competing in the theological and literary worlds of her time. Her masculine pen name increased the power she needed in order to be all she wanted to be, not running and hiding, just embracing life as she saw it, and in the era in which she saw it.

No waiting for a rain of roses for her.

Today consider if you are waiting for a rain of roses.

New Eyes

The real voyage of discovery consists not in seeking new landscapes, but in having new eyes.

—Marcel Proust

A significant challenge to any seminar presenter is the problem of follow-up or continuity: What is going to allow the participants to keep their new insights fresh and accessible? What would keep the information from fading into the fog of forgetting, which the passage of time seems to engender? It's typical for participants to leave the seminar with the best of intentions and enthusiasm, and just as typical for participants to lose them in a few weeks.

One response to this challenge is to base the seminar on the skill of having new eyes. If you leave with new eyes, the follow-up problem takes care of itself; everything you see from now on will be a new discovery.

You will have a new and different way of seeing something that you have been looking at all your life.

Something such as "doing nothing": Today I am going to use new eyes with which to see "doing nothing."

For today, please see time spent doing nothing not with your old eyes, not as a waste of time, not as boring, not as unproductive, not as guilt-ridden laziness. Now, please see it with new eyes, as very fertile time, as urgently necessary and life-giving time, in which to wake up and remember who you are.

See it as the most important time of your life.

The problem of follow-up disappears when you have new eyes.

Today bring new eyes, rather than new landscapes, to what you want to discover.

Road Rage

There is no class of person more moved by hate than the motorist.

—C. R. Hewitt

I wonder if you have the same experience that I sometimes do. I'm driving along, thinking that I am in a fine mood, when the driver waiting at a stoplight in front of me puts on his left turn signal just as the light turns green. The reaction is immediate and strong: I am absolutely furious! I struggle not to lay on the horn and do a few other things as well.

How can I go from serenity to rage in an instant? And because of such a thing as a left turn? Can't I really afford the thirty seconds or minute that I'll have to wait? What happened? What's going on in me?

The only answer I can come up with is that the car has become a symbol of so many of the societal frustrations we experience today. The classic symbol of our independence now often thwarts our progress and becomes an inconvenience and a limit on our freedom, not a means to it.

For a serene life, we need to pay a lot of attention to driving automobiles, whether or not we actually drive.

I propose spending some time getting to know your car—well, not your car, really, but getting to know yourself in your car. Think about how you want to react to other drivers, talk to family members and friends about your common experiences while driving, and perhaps change your expectations of what driving will actually be like for you—more traffic, more delays, more jams.

And if the rage hits you anyway, remember to take a deep breath or two—always do that. Then see what you can come up with to restore serenity. I try to think of the fact that I'm only one of many trying to get somewhere. And if I'm feeling particularly honest, I recall that sometimes I am the one putting on the left turn signal just as the light turns green.

Spend some time with your car today.

two

Making Room
for Life

Something from Nothing

One of the greatest necessities in America
Is to discover creative solitude.
　　　　　　　　—Carl Sandburg

When our creative thinking has come to a halt and our thoughts are caught in fruitless repetitive circles, it is time to stop and allow our minds to meander.

This was certainly true for Elias Howe, who lived in the mid-1800s and is credited with inventing the sewing machine. The story goes that one day, as he was working on the sewing machine project, he became particularly frustrated. He had been working with a regular sewing needle and had tried many different ways to mechanize it, with no success.

He decided to take a break from his efforts and sat at the window of his workshop, gazing out in reverie. He later told his wife what happened:

As I wandered in my mind, a remarkable scene came to me. I was in a deep jungle and I was in a big, black pot with a roaring fire under it. I was being cooked alive! A warrior came at me with spear raised and ready to thrust.

But what I noticed at that moment was something very curious about the spear: It had a hole in its tip.

The pivotal discovery in the invention of the sewing machine is that the hole for the thread goes in the tip of the needle, not at its other end, as in a regular needle. The breakthrough had eluded the inventor in his conscious intellectual efforts, but came to him poetically, graphically, in his moment of reverie.

Creativity thrives on doing nothing. In the moments that might seem empty, what has been there all along in some embryonic form is given space and comes to life.

Today, bring the gift of doing nothing to your challenges that need creative solutions.

What's Going on Here?

Things are seldom about what they seem to be about.
—George Wilson, S.J.

Sometimes we are so focused on accomplishing one particular task that our vision narrows and we overlook the obvious cause of pain and distress in those around us.

Joey, fifteen, was almost literally dragged by his mother into my office at the social service agency where I was family counselor intern.

"He absolutely refuses to go to school," she said to me, clearly frustrated.

The three of us spent the session in different ways: I was trying to figure out the cause of his school phobia. The mother spent the session expressing frustration at her once cooperative son. The boy spent the session in disgruntled silence, with a couple of one-syllable exceptions.

To all my questions they responded with very little information. I couldn't figure out what was at the heart of the problem.

At the end I said, "Is there anything else you can tell me about all of this?"

"No," they agreed.

"Well, let's meet again next week and maybe by then we'll be able to do better," I concluded.

"Oh, no," the mother said, "we can't come back. We're in the midst of packing. Next week the family's moving to Philadelphia."

Finally I got it! Of course Joey was upset about leaving home and moving across the country. We extended the session and gave the boy a chance to express his grief at losing all his friends and his mother a chance to understand how difficult that is.

This family was moving so fast that they missed the obvious. They needed to slow down to notice. Maybe in Philadelphia.

When conflict arises today take a moment to ask: What is this conversation (comment, request, et cetera) really about?

What We Often Miss

Sometimes I go about in pity for myself, and all the while a great wind is bearing me across the sky.

—Ojibwa saying

As you might guess, I love epigraphs, those pithy sayings that capture an important idea in a few, happy words. Each of these reflections begins with an epigraph. There are many that I like, but if I had to choose my favorite, on many days I would choose the one above.

Consider the magnificence of the moments when we remember the Ojibwa saying. Any of the moments of your life can become a wonder, any situation you're in can be affected by transcendent joy.

The two of us are in the grocery store, doing the shopping for the week. We are a bit annoyed with each other. You pick out some things, I others. There are a few questions—"Do we have enough milk? How many bagels should we get?"—but mostly we are both focused on what we are doing; our care for each other is not expressed in clear ways. Actually, I am feeling sorry for myself, having to put

35

up with your moods. (But remember, a great wind is bearing us right now dramatically, miraculously across the sky!)

Some friends have stopped by at a very inconvenient time. I have planned a couple of projects that I've wanted to do for a long time. I am trying to be nice, trying to be patient. I wish they would go. I wish they never came. (But remember, a magnificent wind is enfolding us all in its arms and bearing us—imagine!—across the sky!)

Especially when you're feeling sorry for yourself, let your pity be a trigger for a Stillpoint that will transport you across the sky.

Today, be awake to the Great Wind in the midst of stress or routine.

Doing and Being

If you are what you do, when you don't you aren't.
—Quoted by William Byron, S.J.

A middle-aged married couple find themselves trying to deal with a less than perfect marriage. In their discussion the wife asks her husband, a physician, why he spends so much time at work. "What is it you get at work that you don't get at home?"

Her husband answers, "When I'm at work it's the only time I feel like I know who I really am."

Being a doctor has become who he is, not just what he does. When he is at home there is no need for a doctor, but much need for a husband, father, homemaker, family man, caregiver, short-order cook, Mr. Fix-it, neighbor, playmate, friend, and so on. But he is a doctor and thus cannot respond with any enthusiasm or authenticity to all his other roles.

If he could learn to see that doctoring is something he does, that it is his work, as well as possibly a source of much of joy and fulfillment, then he could be free to do lots of other things as well, and just be himself. As it is, when he returns home he is still a doctor. Most of the time nobody there needs a doctor. So he floats around unengaged, bored, and causing trouble.

Doing nothing can help you if you find yourself in the doctor's situation. Be still and be with yourself. By *doing nothing* the *doing* part of you drops away and the *being* part of you gradually comes alive. It has to, because the doing is gone.

The irony is that the more you separate what you are from what you do, the more you can do!

Consider: If you were no longer to do what you do, who would you be?

Getting to the True Self

*The mind can only reflect the true image of the Self
when it is tranquil and wholly relaxed.*
                                        —Indira Gandhi

My client was worried. Her mother, a widow of about sixty, had become ill quite suddenly. My client was the only available relative and thus responsible for her mother's care.

When she came in for her weekly session, my client's main concern was about the surgeon who was to operate on her mother. When she tried to make an appointment with this doctor to learn about the procedure, this is what she experienced: It was difficult to get to the doctor; he had gatekeepers with endless excuses. But he also had a reputation of being a good surgeon.

When she did finally get a moment of his time, she experienced him as impatient, stressed, self-impressed, and not at all relaxed. His smile was forced, too quick, and seemed insincere. He didn't look her in the eye while speaking to her, and he had to check his notes for her mother's name and condition.

My client went home and spent about an hour in quiet reflection. Then she called the surgeon and declined his service.

"I can't believe I did that!" was her comment, "but he just didn't seem present to the moment at all. I felt he was always putting his attention somewhere else, not on me, nor on my mother. I just didn't sense he cared."

The doctor's too-stressed life—and whatever else—did not allow him a tranquil and wholly relaxed mind and thus he did not access what Indira Gandhi calls his own "true image." My client wanted someone who was wholly present to himself to operate on her mother. So would I.

No matter how busy you are, spend relaxing time today to give life to your true self.

Clarity of Intention

Fat ... addicted ... broke ... a house full of junk ... and no time.

—Mary Pipher

That's how families end up if they merely allow the dominant culture to happen to them. The implication is clear. We are called to face the culture proactively, to practice intentional living, to be active and not merely reactive, and to want, along with Thoreau, "to live deliberately."

When we are quiet, we become more clear about what we know and what we value. We don't accept whatever the unthinking voices of the world happen to tell us. That's the effect of being awake and remembering who you are. We are able to live on purpose, intentionally rather than by rote.

Consider:

We are naive if we think that "advertising doesn't affect me, I just don't listen."

We are misguided if we conclude that "false claims are harmless, everyone makes them."

We will often be hoodwinked if we accept and believe whatever we are told, by whatever authority, without critique.

We are dangerously deceived if we allow someone (or some group, or institution) to think for us, to make decisions for us.

Mary Pipher, an experienced family counselor, speaks these very strong words from experience. She has seen people allow themselves to become addicted and put to sleep by acquiring a house full of junk, and who have no time for what, if awakened, they would consider really important to them.

Today, think about how much of your life is on automatic pilot and how much is intentional.

Prayer Break

It's a kind of reality check.

—Shahed Amanullah

All of us at one time or another experience the unwelcome feelings of anxiety and worry. Indeed, if we believe statistics on stress, for many people these two feelings are common companions. Not that we need statistics; our lives and those of our families and friends are testimonies.

In yesterday's newspaper, there was an article about the stress of people who are members of religious minorities. The article pointed out how often they are misunderstood because of public ignorance of their religion. The man quoted above, a Muslim living in an American city, is named as an example. He is presented in the article as a bright but average guy for whom his faith is a practical part of life. He is a project engineer with a local transportation company.

On Fridays, the Muslim Sabbath, he takes an hour for *juma* prayers at his mosque. This is what he says of his practice: "It is a kind of reality check. You pause what you are doing and remember why you're here, what your purpose is and who to be thankful for."

This is his response—at least one of them—to stress: a prayer break. His words capture not only the spirit, but practically the definition of Stopping: to be aware and to remember. And clearly the practice gives him support at a time of trial.

What are the stresses that the world causes for you? Would a prayer break also bring you support and be a way of managing your stress? If so, what would be a prayer break for you? Maybe a visit to a place of worship, a momentary pause and reflection, the reading of a favorite text.

What would a prayer break look like for you today? Do it.

Just Sit

Sometimes I sits and thinks, and sometimes I just sits.
—Satchel Paige

Peple who are at ease with themselves are a wonderful gift to the world. They model for us with a power that words can never match.

When I was a boy, I had Satchel Paige's picture on my wall, along with about fifteen other Cleveland Indian baseball players. Satchel had a special attraction. He not only became the first African American pitcher in the American League (at the age of forty-two), he was also full of joy, wisdom, and showmanship. He just loved life, even though, especially at its beginning, it didn't offer him much.

He could pitch words as well as he could pitch a baseball. The above words are an example. Satchel always had his eye on the crowd and knew how to give them what they wanted, and sometimes what they needed as well.

In my memory of him, I realize that he always had quietness, serenity, and even a sense of slowness about him—even though he was famous for his fastball—almost as if he were always remembering something important, something he didn't want to forget. His smile took a while to complete itself, and he had an easy grace in his movements.

Is there someone in your life who is a model of serenity for you? What gives them such a calm in the storm of life? How can you cultivate that in yourself?

Today, find yourself a model of serenity and make yourself an apprentice.

Oops!

Most men pursue pleasure with such breathless haste they hurry past it.

—Sören Kierkegaard

It seems to be characteristic of the young to rush so fast through life that they miss the best parts. But I seem to have been fairly adept at dragging that youthful characteristic along with me well into my adult years. I still have to remind myself not to hurry past my pleasure. (I often need to give this advice to myself when I am eating: My tendency is to eat too fast and not savor the food, and thus miss the pleasure.)

Businesspeople seem particularly prone to this tendency from my observation. It must be the nature of doing business, competitive and fast, and the fact that the winner—the best in the business—gets the prize of financial success.

Many successful climbers of the corporate ladder later recognize themselves as those who were so intent, so earnest, so hardworking, moving with such breathless haste up the ladder, that they happened to miss a vital element in their pursuit: the ladder was leaning against the wrong wall.

When they arrive at the top, it hits them. For example, "Oops! I am a top executive, but what I really wanted was to be a writer." Looking back, they can recognize what they had hurried past: the high school teacher who encouraged them to write, the college prize won for essay writing, the longing to create a novel—all missed, hurried past.

Noticing and recognizing pleasures is what we gain from our moments of doing nothing, of reverie, of awakening to our true desires and passions.

It is never too late to find a new wall or climb a different ladder.

Do you have an "Oops" to say about what you've hurried past?

Thoughts Unsought

The thoughts that often come unsought, and, as it were, drop into the mind, are commonly the most valuable of any we have.

—John Locke

Where do they come from, these unsought thoughts?

Pope John XXIII tells the way he first thought about convening the Second Vatican Council, which has been called the most significant religious event of the century and will influence the world for centuries to come.

He said, although not with Locke's words, that the idea for the Council just dropped into his mind. It did not come as a logical answer to a particular problem. It just dropped in, so to speak. Lawrence Elliott, in his biography of the popular pope, quotes him: "Suddenly an inspiration sprang up within us as a flower that blooms in an unexpected springtime... a council!"

I won't attempt to answer the question about where these ideas come from. But let me say something about not missing them when they do come. And not just to popes.

We won't miss these gems only if we have prepared ourselves in advance of their visit by creating a place of welcome, if we have a sign on our souls saying: Valuable Unsought Thoughts—Enter Here.

The construction of the sign includes the wood of silence, the metal of serenity, and the nails of quiet recollection.

Pope John is a fine example of such a soul. His autobiography reveals a lifelong desire and effort to "know and do God's will." When the thought of the Council dropped in, his place of welcome was ready, having been prepared by prayer, service, humility, and many hours and days of contemplation.

See your quiet moments today as preparation of a welcoming place for valuable thoughts that will just drop in.

Opening to Angels

What is knocking at the door at night? Is it somebody who wants to do us harm?

—Friedrich Hölderlin

One of the gifts that comes from quiet time is openness to receive what is offered to you. But tagging along on the heels of openness, of course, is vulnerability. It's just the nature of things that when you are open, you are vulnerable. You won't miss the wonders that are available, but you can also get hurt, or become overwhelmed. It's a risk.

Here is a recent experience of my friend Bob: He had just taken his assigned seat on the aisle in the rear of the packed airplane and was getting settled when a man approached him and said, "You're in my seat, you'll have to move." Bob checked his ticket and saw that he was indeed in the seat the ticket indicated.

The man in turn produced a ticket with the same seat number and said in a loud voice, "Well, you have to move to some other seat. I always sit here and I am going to sit here now." All eyes and ears were focused on what was becoming a small scene.

Bob, standing by now, considered his options. When the flight attendant approached, he said, "If this man wants to sit here, that's fine, I'll sit somewhere else."

Gloating, the man forthwith took the seat while the flight attendant—in a slightly raised voice—said to Bob, "Thank you, sir. There is a free seat in first class, please follow me."

Bob followed his desire to be cooperative and peaceful and took a risk of being seen as the loser in an argument.

The opening quote above has a continuation: "No, no, it is not somebody who wants to harm us. It is three strange angels. Admit them."

My friend Bob took the risk and didn't miss the angels. He would not have missed the angels even if there were no free seat in first class.

Watch for three strange angels today (or maybe just one … or five).

three

Remembering to Take the Time

A Lesson from Sister

Sit down, be still, and pay attention!
—Sister Mary Odilo

I can still hear my seventh grade teacher's voice: "David, go to your place! Be still and pay attention!" She didn't say "Be quiet!" but always "Be still!", which implies not only a lack of noise but a lack of movement as well, a quietude of the whole person.

You have long since left the realm of schoolchildren, but these words are just as important—no, more important—because now you can know their real power: Practicing stillness and attention can change your life, especially as your practice gains power and effectiveness.

Here are a few questions to consider:

What is your way of being still? In which place are you likely to be when you are still—inside, outside, in a particular room or space? In what posture would you tend to be—sitting, standing, lying down?

Are you someone for whom being still is particularly difficult or challenging? Could you practice being still while walking?

When you are indeed still, to what is your attention drawn? How do you think about paying attention? That is, what does it mean to you?

Armed with this description of what paying attention looks like for you, you won't miss the opportunities to practice it. You will be ready when the moments for stillness come.

Today pick a few moments to sit down, be still, and pay attention.

Telephones, Beepers, and Clocks

Never send to know for whom the bell tolls; it tolls for thee.
–John Donne

The most frequent challenge I hear from busy people who want to find peace in their daily lives is that they have goodwill, but they just plain forget to take a few moments for a Stillpoint. At the end of the day they realize they only did one or two, or even none.

What helps me, and many of the people I speak with, is finding triggers. Look for the triggers in your day—moments, people, situations, times, places, events, goings, comings—that have these traits in common: (1) They are frequent. (2) They are automatic. (3) They are consistent.

Here is an example: telephones, beepers, and clocks, or—putting a spin on John Donne's words—bells that sound in your environment. When you hear them, you can Stop, take a breath, and remember who you are—every time you hear the phone, the clock, the doorbell, or a beeper.

Here's one I do. Every time I hear the microwave beeper—a sound I find annoying—I call myself to a momentary breath of relaxation and a recollection of how I'll enjoy whatever is being warmed.

Here are a few helps to establish an event or a sound as a trigger. Place sticky notes or other signs on things; put things "out of place" to remind you; take a few moments at the beginning of the day and put your Stillpoints in your imagination: *When I take a bathroom break, I will stay there for one minute longer, close my eyes and notice what I am feeling physically in my body or emotionally.*

It takes a while to establish the practice, so don't get discouraged. Stick with it. If you do, I'll guarantee you will become good at it and, more important, the quality of your day will leap forward.

> *Right now, think of two triggers in your day—bells that toll for thee.*

Breathe!

Our breath is the bridge from our body to our mind.
—Thich Nhat Hanh

It is impossible to overemphasize the importance of deep, conscious breathing. Its benefits are numerous and profound, far beyond what one might expect from an activity so common and automatic.

The tendency in our speeded-up world is to breathe shallow, quick breaths that contribute to our general feeling of tightness and hurry.

As you breathe in, close your eyes and allow the breath to gently push your stomach out, pause there for a brief moment, then breathe out as your stomach returns to normal. As you breathe out, allow your jaw and shoulders to drop in an easy manner. Relax and feel the relaxation flow from the top of your head down to your fingertips. Stay still for a moment and then repeat the breathing.

Remember to breathe this way as often as you can. Every breath can bring us to a moment of peace and tranquillity.

Remember especially when you are nervous, upset, angry, stressed, on stage, concentrating, rushed, or in so many other tense moments that seem so frequent these days.

As the Vietnamese monk and teacher Thich Nhat Hanh reminds us, when we breathe, there is an automatic connection between soul and body; we are brought to an awareness of our spiritual natures by the physical act of breathing.

"Things to do today: Exhale, inhale, exhale. Ahhh." (Jack Kornfield)

Pick a Day for a Stopover

Seize the day!

—Horace

Today I issue you a challenge: It's a very practical way to put into practice Horace's encouragement. Sit down with your calendar and seize the day! Pick out a day within a few months during which you will do a Stopover, that is, a whole day in which you will do nothing. I know it might be scary. You probably think you're too busy. But I am encouraging you to take a risk and try it. I'm fairly sure that the experience will be such that you will want to do it again and again.

Chose a day during which you are sure you will have nothing else you must do. Then mark that day on your calendar with a big *S* for your time of creatively doing nothing.

As the day approaches, you can anticipate it, wondering, for example, "What in the world will I do with all that time with nothing to do?" (Answer: nothing). Resist planning anything except perhaps going to some place that will facilitate your Stopover, like a beach, a park, or a retreat house. Or just plan to stay home. Make a determination to stay with it.

Remember to prepare the other people in your life. Too often, they will not encourage you, finding many reasons why this does not sound like a good idea, or even seems a little weird. You'll probably find that the idea pushes people's limits a bit. Remind them from time to time that your Stopover day is coming. It might be best to refer to it simply as some quiet time. Find ways and places to assure you will not be disturbed.

When the planning is finished you can just look forward with anticipation!

Today: Mark an S (for seize!) on a day in your calendar for a Stopover.

Going Within

If you aren't used to going within, you will need to be patient with yourself....

—Barbara De Angelis

A Stillpoint involves ceasing what you are doing, breathing, and turning your focus within yourself. Some of us are quite comfortable going within ourselves, and do it regularly; others are not so comfortable and find the process daunting and unfamiliar. If you are in the latter group please heed the advice above and be patient with yourself. Keep in mind a few ideas:

This need not be complicated. The going in does not have to be an active searching for something, but rather simply an awareness, a quiet looking. It is more passive than active. Just being still.

You probably focus within regularly but just don't call it that. You might find, with naturalist John Muir, that "going out [into Nature]... was really going in."

Remember to breathe.

Here are a few thoughts to help you get started going within:

What feeling do I notice right now? (Try not to answer what you are thinking.)

Can I pick a word or two which would come close to describing the current state of my soul?

Name a few virtues you know are yours (such as kindness, goodwill, empathy. . .). Does one describe what you see inside yourself now?

Throughout the day today, turn your focus in to become more awake.

Remembering Who You Are

Remember that thou are dust, and unto dust thou shall return.

—from the liturgy of Ash Wednesday

The priest or minister in some Christian traditions uses these words as he rubs ashes on your forehead on the first day of Lent, Ash Wednesday. They are meant to help us remember death. It gets right to the point. Ideally, such remembering calls one to a conversion of life, puts things in perspective, so that first things are indeed first, last things last.

But we have more things to remember than the fact that we will die: what we desire, who we love, what we have chosen as goals and ideals, where we've come from, where we're going, who we want with us, the road we're taking, what we need for the journey, our ultimate values, what is most meaningful, and so on.

Remembering is the part of the Stillpoint when you call to mind something meaningful. But the nature of a Stillpoint is to be brief, so the remembering often is a concentrated or abbreviated expression that stands for the reality it symbolizes. Here are some examples:

A word, or a few words: Patience. Relax. Peace. Home. Be here now. *Memento mori.* I am with you. I can do it.

An image of a sacred place, a spiritual leader, a family member, a symbol, an event, a prayer.

A value, an ideal, a virtue in a gesture, such as clasping your hands, extending your arms, bowing your head, raising your eyes, touching index finger with thumb to create a circle.

An intention-for-the-day that you made in the morning.

What are the things you want to remember? By making them a part of your daily Stillpoints, think of all the remembering you can do in a year!

Determine what you want to remember today during your Stillpoints. Pick a symbol to express it.

Opening

Open all your pores and bathe in all the tides of nature.
—Henry David Thoreau

When we take daily time to remember who we are and what is important to us, we can be more open to life. If we are not open, we miss so much! Being open means the realities of life have a way to get into you, the gates are open, and you won't miss what you don't want to miss.

One of the ways to open all your pores is to find an image that signifies opening to you. An image is instantaneous, takes little effort, and has a powerful effect on us. (A picture is worth a thousand words.)

Here are a few examples of images of openness that might get you started in finding your own:

A dish antenna: open to all the signals of the universe

A sapling: stretching to reach the sun and rain

A whale, huge maw agape and swimming through the krill

A magnet: attracting your opposites

A child: knowing that everything is possible

When we race through life never stopping, openness is difficult because too much goes right through us, without making any difference in our lives.

In the words quoted above, Thoreau uses the analogy of bathing. Perhaps that could be the image for you: When you are immersed in a tub or standing under a steady shower of water, no part of you is missed. You are open.

Pick a metaphor for openness (perhaps from the list above). Three times today stop and recall your image.

The Chatter Just Keeps Going

---

*Perhaps what becomes most clear when we do nothing
is that thought keeps on going, as though we were doing
something.*

—Steven Harrison

In our attempts to be still, often our internal chatter does not stop but goes on nattering away, and
we are often stymied in our efforts to thwart it. Can
you really stop everything? Is it possible literally to
do nothing? Probably not. The doing nothing that
I'm talking about is, as author Steven Harrison says,
"a surprisingly active place." No matter how we try
to empty our minds and clear out all our thoughts,
something always seems to be going on there.

This is a commonly mentioned challenge to any
process that would attempt to achieve a quiet mind:
"I can get my body to be still, all right, but how do
I stop my mind?" I can only pass on the advice learned
from the experience of the wise, and that I continue
to give myself:

First, don't let this discourage you. It is a universal challenge.

Focus on your breathing. Always return to your breath. This is the fundamental response for achieving a quiet mind.

Allow the chatter to come in, notice it, and allow it to continue out, thus creating a flow rather than a dam.

Try silently reciting a mantra: a meaningful and oft-repeated word, brief phrase, or prayer.

Sometimes it may help to practice several, short periods of stillness—Stillpoints—rather than longer ones. Chatter has less of a chance to intrude.

And last, to repeat, don't let it discourage you. It is a universal challenge!

Notice today if chatter interrupts your quiet moments and what response seems most effective for you.

Filling In

We yearn for a moment's peace and quiet, only to turn on the radio, make a phone call, or run an errand as soon as an opportunity for solitude presents itself.

—Ronnie Polanezcky

Picture yourself at your moments of transition, especially when they are sudden or quick or involve dramatic change: As you move from the frantic pace of work to the quiet pace of home (or, indeed, its opposite); as you leave a day of solitary work to join a large group of talking people; as you move from the loudness of a fifth-grade classroom to the silence of the walk home; as you move from a bustling city to a country village; as you face a solitary life after a long life of companionship.

Each transition brings with it a feeling of unfamiliarity and a moment of disorientation. Too often the first inclination is to fill the gap with some kind of commotion, even though, as the quote above indicates, we often profess to yearn for peace and quiet.

It is very easy for me to recall times that I have filled in these awkward moments, these from-to's, with an activity that distracts me from what is going on. Invariably I regret it.

Today I encourage you simply to sit through whatever period of transition you are going through. Stay there a moment. Notice what is going on for you, acknowledge the disorientation and bring all your attention to the present. For instance, arriving home after work, instead of racing in the door, turning on the radio, and picking up the phone, just stay in your car (or on the front step, just outside the front door) for two minutes. The world will not collapse if you take two minutes.

Now you will better know what you need, and how you want to deal with this new time in your life, and you'll be a little more prepared to cope with the new state of being.

Today notice your moments of peace, and if your impulse is to fill them.

Gaze out the Window

What is life if, full of care,
We have no time to stand and stare?
—W. H. Davies

So many influences of contemporary life seem to militate against our remaining awake and aware of what is meaningful to us. So much seems to clamor for our attention and keep us from being present to the moment. Everything seems to shout, "Look at me!" or worse, "Look at me right now!"

As an antidote to those demands of life, I invite you to stand and stare, or simply to gaze. Perhaps gaze out the window right now and allow whatever is in your field of vision simply to be there. (Lacking a window, simply gaze about you.) Just let your gaze fall easily upon what is outside the window or what is around you for a moment. Most likely, what you see is ordinary to you; you've seen it many times.

Now notice what is there. Noticing brings you from the general view of gazing to a more specific way to see. You note the weather or the temperature.

You notice the time of day and the light. You take note of the things or people within your vision.

Now allow your noticing to call you to a quiet moment. Is the weather cool? What does cool weather lead you to? Is the sun shining? Who is the light of your life? Are we in spring? Is there something budding in your life? Is it a morning scene? What do you want to feel at day's end?

When one of life's voices rudely shouts at you, "Look at me!" respond by standing and staring or with an easy gaze out the window. Then notice the ordinary but noble things you see there.

There are so many opportunities for standing and staring, for gazing and noticing.

Today begin a new custom: Gaze out the window and notice....

Pacing

We seem to move forward, but we don't go anywhere; we are not being drawn by a goal. Thus we smile....

       –Thich Nhat Hanh

Moving forward and not going anywhere, walking but not with any goal: these are paradoxes that seem to go against wisdom, at least the conventional kind.

In the hospital waiting room a worried, nervous, expectant father paces back and forth, back and forth.

A monk walks the circle of the monastery closure, moving slowly and reading the psalms of his daily prayer. He could sit in the chapel to pray, but today he does not.

Sarah paces around her small office—four steps in this direction, four steps in that—for fifteen minutes, staring at the floor. She is perplexed and anxious. The pacing soothes her.

I am walking the labyrinth in Grace Cathedral in San Francisco. It is a large circle on the floor of the grand, gothic-style cathedral, with a clear and winding path to the center and out again. The purpose of the walking is spiritual. I arrive at the center quieted, spend some moments there, and return to the outer world refreshed.

Pacing is walking a predetermined, repetitive path. It's quite different from taking a walk because it frees the body from having to consider and adapt to the nature of the terrain. It frees the mind from making choices about what direction to take.

Pacing is a wonderful paradox: We are indeed moving forward, but we are not going anywhere. And thus, says the Buddhist monk, we smile.

When it's hard to stay still, but you need to be quiet, remember to pace.

Quieting Your Day

Silence is a receptive space.

—Barbara De Angelis

A great way to become open, and stay open, is simply to be quiet and receptive to what might be:

Be still.

Breathe.

Relax.

Breathe again.

And again.

Let a little time pass, doing nothing.

Slowly the space you are in becomes open, receptive. Slowly, you realize that you can trust the quiet, nothing will scare or overwhelm you. Slowly you begin to realize that this is a time of receiving, not just of emptying. Slowly.

Now again:

Be still.

Breathe.

Relax.

Breathe again.

And again.

Let a little time pass, doing nothing.

Now note how you are feeling at the end of that little practice. Give the feeling a name, like Tranquillity or Composure. And when the time comes for you to get going again, bring Tranquillity or Composure with you. Name it to yourself from time to time during the day and revisit the feeling.

Do this a few times today.

four

Finding
Your Balance

Balance

In the depths of winter, I finally learned that within me
there lay an invincible summer.

−Albert Camus

The more I age, the more I know that the spiritual path—life viewed primarily through the prism of our meanings and values—must involve paradox, confusion, dead ends, and shadowed places that are often foul to behold. Any path that tries to avoid these will get us into trouble.

As tempting as it may be, a life lived as if all were beautiful and happy—or could be, if only we knew just how to do it!—is a life doomed either to much unnecessary frustration or to ineffective and lightweight surface skimming.

In the summer, there are always the seeds of winter. When you're down, up will come. In the joy of success dwell the seeds of failure. In moments of bleakest grief shines the light of new energy and life. The dark and the bright, the joyful and the sad, the pleasure and the pain, life and death, death and resurrection.

Now please don't count me among those who don't like to emphasize the good and the happy aspects of life. I was raised, after all, on Johnny Mercer singing, "You gotta ac-*cennn*-tuate the positive, e-*limmm*-inate the negative . . . and don't mess with Mister In-between!"

Isn't the goal to embrace life *just as it really is?* And for that we need time of quiet, time with nothing to distract us, time for just being in the moment. Otherwise we may give in to avoiding or denying anything that we don't find easy or happy.

Today, look for the summer in your winter (or the winter in your summer).

Mowing the Lawn

Everyone thinks I'm crazy not to get a sit-down mower.
—radio host

I was a guest author on a National Public Radio program and in the course of our conversation the interviewer said to me: "Let me tell you why I don't get one of those big sit-down lawn mowers, but keep my old small one. First, it uses less gas, but really it's because when I am walking behind my old lawn mower, I am in a different space. For some reason I just feel different—quiet, peaceful—and I like it."

I'm glad he didn't let anyone talk him into getting a new lawn mower. Walking along behind his lawn mower is his time of serenity, his quiet time—yes, even with the lawn mower's racket—his time for himself, and his over-busy life does not allow for much of it.

Often, we do in fact have times of quiet and peace, times of doing nothing, but we just don't identify them as such. It helps to identify them, because then we will value them more clearly and defend them more staunchly. What are those times for you? Swimming laps? Doing dishes? Digging in the garden? The more we recognize how we find those times of peace and serenity already in our lives, the more we can be conscious in choosing them.

And remember to look for your serenity where you might not expect to find it, like walking along behind a noisy mower.

Today notice some valued, but previously unidentified, times of doing nothing.

Stop and Smell the Roses

Don't hurry, don't worry. You're only here for a short visit. So be sure to stop and smell the flowers.

—Walter C. Hagen

Somehow "flowers" got changed to "roses" but Walter Hagen's words—and especially the idea behind them—are still familiar to us hassled, harried, contemporary folks. An early legend of American golf, Hagen played in the 20s and 30s and is considered the first professional golfer.

Golf is a good way to understand the importance of Hagen's words. I am not a golfer, although I have played a few rounds in my life. What strikes me about golf is the relatively short time given to actually hitting the ball. If playing eighteen holes takes about three hours, I'm guessing that during about five minutes of that three hours you are actually hitting the golf ball. That's one thirty-sixth of the time.

Thirty-five thirty-sixths is for smelling the roses: walking, noticing, maybe occasional conversation, being aware of the weather and other expressions of the natural world—grass, trees, sand (!), perhaps water.

Golf is time-out. No one has access to you on the golf course. (Or they didn't until cell phones and beepers, that is. I've heard of courses where they're banned). You're just walking the Earth, and every once in a while hitting a ball with a club.

Golf, played in this leisurely way, also expresses one's belief in Hagen's words, "You're only here for a short visit." Playing a round of golf can help you put into practice your agreement with Hagen's sentiments. But then there's also fishing....

Do you enjoy an activity—like golf—during which you can find serenity?

A Walk Down the Street

I took a walk on Spaulding's farm the other afternoon. I saw the setting sun lighting up the opposite side of a stately pine wood.

—Henry David Thoreau

I took a walk down my street yesterday and noticed a few things:

There are those two very yellow houses right next to each other, the only yellow houses on the block.

The elms are not showing the slightest bit of green and here it's already the middle of April.

There goes the woman who runs with wolves, a serious runner accompanied by four equally serious wolves, although they are probably wolflike dogs. I enjoy her energy.

Just noticing various things as you walk down your street can be more powerful than it might seem. The noticing—paying attention to what you see, hear, feel, taste, and smell—brings you into the present time and place and takes you out of worry, planning, and anxiety.

As I return to my work I feel refreshed, renewed.

Walking is treading upon the Earth. Thus I remember my humanity, my place on the Earth, my belonging. I imagine the curve of the Earth and the small part of the curve I traverse.

I have also noticed that my walking brings me some practical benefits. Sometimes an image of what I recently noticed on my walk will be just what I needed as a symbol or metaphor for what I am trying to express. The yellow houses in fact reminded me of something that I had meant to do recently but had forgotten.

For the most part, however, just walk. The rest will take care of itself.

Walk down your street today. What do you notice?

Really Nothing New

Dolce far niente!

—old Italian saying

At the end of one of my seminars, I was about to thank people for coming and ask if there were any more questions or ideas. There seemed to be none so I had begun to say good-night when from the very back of the room I caught a glimpse of someone waving a hand tentatively. Even from a distance, I could tell it was a hand that had seen many seasons.

I acknowledged the wave, "Yes, someone in the back?"

Very slowly an old man came out from his seat into the aisle and walked a little way toward the front. He was smiling.

"I have enjoyed your talk," he said, "and what you say is most important, but it is really nothing new. When I was a boy in Italy I learned the importance of one of our favorite sayings: *Dolce far niente.* How sweet it is to do nothing."

He paused, then said it again, slowly, with a great deal of feeling, and a strong, careful gesture, making

89

it obvious that he not only believed it, but had lived it: *"Dolce far niente!"*

Certainly, the idea of intentionally spending deliberate time doing nothing in order to find peace and serenity is nothing new. It is part of literally every major religious and spiritual tradition, as well as often a part of many national and regional cultures. I particularly like the Italian one mentioned here. In just three beautiful words there is such joy and feeling.

Can you identify a part of one of your traditions—religious, ethnic, cultural, linguistic—that encourages doing nothing on purpose?

Simplifying Prayer

The more simple we are, the more complete we become.
–attributed to August Rodin

The simpler, the more complete? Rodin's words become clearer, more powerful, when you think of his sculptures—*The Thinker,* for example, or his portrayal of John the Baptist. The simple, clear, strong lines, free of much fine detail, capture an essence.

So many of us stay away from prayer because we are convinced that we don't really know how to do it, or there are certain ways it should be done, or certain results should occur, or only certain kinds of believing people should pray.

But prayer is simply an attitude of the heart that desires communication with the divine, however it is found. It is utterly simple. Both for those who think and pray in terms of a specific God as well as for those who don't, prayer informs and transforms our lives.

Consider:

Who changes with prayer? Is it not the one praying?

Why pray? Is it not, like in any relationship, to be in touch?

Is one type of prayer better than another type? Or is it a question of how do I need to pray right now?

Is there any right way to pray? Any wrong way?

Prayer is an attitude of the heart. It can be expressed in myriad ways. There is no limit. There are no boundaries. We must not worry at all about the details of prayer, but only the essence of connecting. Let go of concern about how well or how long or how wisely you pray.

Kahlil Gibran reminds us, "There is a desire within us that drives [us]. . . to the divine." Allow the desire to have its way, to be in control, to lead you to new ways to pray.

The simpler the prayer, the more complete.

Notice today how often you are, indeed, praying.

Still Life

In the dead of winter, I'd been longing for Life, Still Life.
—Eileen Smith

Columnist and theologian Smith was hoping for some snow. As for many of us, the holidays are wonderful for her, but too often they become the "get ready, get set, GO holidays." And now, the holidays over, she faced: "Schedules. Deadlines. Carpools. Too much to do and not enough time to do it in." What she needed was some snow.

One evening she and her children prayed for snow; the children wanted school canceled, she wanted life to be still.

"[The next] morning met us with wonder. It stopped us in our tracks. Its beauty took our breath away. Everything dusted in white.... Everything quiet.... Snow is spread out like an endless blanket... wrapping us all in the welcome gift of 'Just Stop.' Just stop rushing. Just stop racing. Just stop running from one thing to another. Slow down. Let go. Breathe. And Just Stop. Just Be. Be still. Be quiet. Be.

"And so, we did. We had no choice. Which is sometimes the best choice of all."

Before the snow, Smith was feeling the effects of the "hard days" of the give and take of family life when, "We forget who we are. Who we are supposed to be.... Sometimes we even unravel. We wonder: Will we ever be whole again?... In the dead of winter, I'd been longing for life, 'Still Life.'"

What can be "snow" for you today? Watch for opportunities to stop and play with people you love and whose company you enjoy. And make it a rule: When something is canceled, rained out, or snowed in, seek your Still Life.

Look for "snow" today and discover your
Still Life.

In the Sunshine

Keep your face to the sunshine and you cannot see the shadow.

—attributed to Helen Keller

Read Helen Keller's words again. What do they mean to you?

I am fond of this aphorism because it seems to me that it can mean two very different—maybe even opposing—things. Let me paraphrase each one.

First interpretation: Keep looking on the bright side of life, emphasizing the positive, and then you will not even notice the negative and painful parts in the shadow. If you keep your face toward the welcome sun, you won't even notice the unwelcome shadow.

Second interpretation: Watch out, because if you only see the bright side of things, you will miss the dark side, which can then do you harm. If you only look at the sunny side, you'll miss what the shadow side has to offer you.

Here is an opportunity to practice both/and rather

than either/or. We don't have to affirm one and deny the other. We can use either, both, or neither.

There are days I need the sunshiny encouragement of the first interpretation, and other days I need the shadowy warning of the second. There are whole periods of life when I need one more than the other. There are also times with neither one hits me as significant.

Which of the two truths is best for you right now? Or do you need them both, but in different parts of your life? Or not at all?

Today, notice the sunshine, notice the shadow. Which do you need more now?

Curbing Forgetfulness

There is a secret bond between slowness and memory,
between speed and forgetting.

—Milan Kundera

What strikes me when I read Kundera's quote is the word *secret*. These are secret bonds. With some moments of reflection, the truth of the whole statement is fairly evident, but why are these bonds secret?

My guess is that they are secret because we have not noticed them before. As recently as a generation ago, these bonds were a common, intuitive understanding. People lived their lives with a conscious realization of the balance between slowness and remembering, between speed and forgetting. They knew that leisure was a necessary part of a balanced life. They knew that if you moved too fast you were bound to forget something.

We know it too, but only if we stop to recollect it. Contemporary life does not afford us the intuitive awareness of our forebears. It is, in fact, counterintuitive to a life in balance. Unthinking acceptance of our culture's rate of speed is a terrible, yet common, error. These formerly secret bonds must now be noticed with full intention, and more, shouted from the rooftops.

If we don't notice the bond between speed and forgetting, we will forget what we need to remember. And we will constantly wonder why life is not working out the way we wanted it to, or why we are always seeking inner peace and not finding it.

One of the secrets about forgetting: You forget that you forgot.

No matter what today's schedule is, don't forget Stillpoints. They curb forgetfulness.

Stress + Relaxation = True Recovery

For every time in stress, you need a recovering time in relaxation.

—Emmett E. Miller, M.D.

Here is a subtle and often misunderstood fact about stress: For every period of stress in your life, you need a corresponding antidote, a period of relaxation, just to maintain your health. To manage stress effectively, you cannot go directly from a stressful situation back to normal life without spending some time in stress-free relaxation. If you neglect the relaxation stage, you will accumulate the effects of stress until they begin to do very serious damage—physical, emotional, and spiritual.

Someone dangerously swerves in front of you on the freeway? Spend some time in specifically restorative relaxation—maybe a long bath, or a half-hour of quiet, or a leisurely walk. Only then return to life as normal.

Your boss yells at you in front of the staff? Find an effective restorative antidote—perhaps a relaxing massage or an enjoyable visit with a friend or mentor. Only then return to life as normal.

Are your children driving you to the breaking point? Try calling a baby-sitter and have an evening out, or enjoy a quiet time with a good novel. Only then return to your normal life.

It is only when you take time for stress-free relaxation that you can *truly* recover from stress; merely returning to life as normal—skipping the relaxation stage—is only apparent recovery.

To change your behavior and begin giving yourself these restorative times of relaxation, try thinking of them as an antidote. That's in fact what they are, an antidote to the poison of stress, which restores you to life in balance.

Today for every little stress, take a little stress-free relaxation.

Action or Rest?

I prefer thought to action, an idea to an event, reflection to activity.

—Honoré de Balzac

It is vain to say human beings ought to be satisfied with tranquillity: They must have action; and they will make it if they cannot find it.

—George Eliot

Well then, which will it be? Activity or some lack of it?

I believe the wisdom called for here is not to chose.

There are times when indeed I do want peace and quiet, but I just can't have it right now. The demands of life forbid it. I must make do with too much action.

And what about the times I call boring? How I yearn for action and something to do, somewhere to go, someone to take me out of this period of ennui!

"To everything there is a season, and a time to every purpose under the heaven," (Ecclesiastes 3). The same biblical text goes on to list such tranquil purposes as healing, crying, mourning, keeping silent, peace, and sewing; and such active pursuits as giving birth, knocking down, dancing, building, and throwing stones. I don't think the biblical writer mentions that we most often don't get to pick the season we want to be in at the moment.

Thus the cycles of our days, our weeks, our months, and our years unfold with times of quiet and times of activity, and most often we don't get to choose the schedule.

Let the resting prepare for the action. Allow the action to promise rest.

In today's action, anticipate rest. In today's rest, prepare for action.

It Just Is

Life just is. You have to flow with it. Give yourself to the moment. Let it happen.

—Jerry Brown

Too sixties? Maybe so. But I believe this sentiment, unlike bell-bottoms and hippies, is a part of the sixties that will stand the test of time. Of course it wasn't new in the sixties, but that decade marked this particular wisdom with its own nuances.

What a difficult lesson to learn! Most often what I do to sabotage this truth is make a judgment. Like last month when I got the worst case of the flu I've ever had. _This shouldn't be happening! I have a trip planned and now I have to cancel it. This is all wrong and I'm very angry that I have the flu. . .and on and on!_

How would I rather respond in that situation? _Whether or not this should happen is not the question. Simply it is. I have the flu and I feel miserable. I have a choice of how to respond. I want to spend my energy in resting and helping my body recover. I don't want to create frustration—and thus stress for me and those around me— where none is necessary or helpful. I want to go with the flow._

"Let it happen" doesn't mean that we can actually let or not let things happen. Most often we have no control: They happen! What it does mean is that I choose how to respond to what is happening.

The martial art of aikido is a perfect example here. It is built upon the principle that if you match the energy and movement of your opponent and go with the flow of it, rather than oppose and fight it, you will accomplish amazing results, as well as conserve energy and keep your balance.

Today quietly observe what keeps you from going with the flow.

Soulbody

All the soarings of my mind begin in my blood.
—Rainer Maria Rilke

Why are we so reluctant to make the connections between the mind and the body? Certainly one of the reasons is that for centuries our Western institutional churches have separated them. I learned very early that I had a soul, and that it could be marked, and that the soul was important and good. And I had a body that was different, less important; it somehow contained the soul. Today I would rather say we are not a soul in a body, nor a body in a soul. We're soulbody.

The underlying assumption in separating and distinguishing the soul from the body is to see the soul as spiritual, good, and eternal. It is separated from the body, which is physical, not so good (maybe even bad), and dies. Ultimately this splitting has put us at war with ourselves.

I have a theory that responds in a very practical way to this unhealthy splitting: When you are experiencing physical malady, it is an indication of spiritual disquiet, and thus its treatment must be spiritual. Conversely, when you are aware of a spiritual malaise, it is a sign that some physical reality needs healing and thus the treatment will be in the bodily realm.

Thus, for a headache, instead of popping pills, take the afternoon off. And for anxiety, rather than a therapy session, get thee to the gym.

The theory can, of course, be carried too far. Aspirin can relieve a headache, and therapy anxiety. But more of a problem is that we don't use the theory at all.

Try it to see if it works for you.

Today: Identify a physical ill and a spiritual healing, or a spiritual ill and a physical healing.

Koyaanisqatsi

*ko-yaa-nis-qatsi: from the Hopi [Native American]
language: n. 1. crazy life. 2. life in turmoil. 3. life
disintegrating. 4. life out of balance. 5. a state of life that
calls for another way of living.*

—from the *Koyaanisqatsi* videocassette jacket

Have you even seen the remarkable film *Koyaanisquatsi?* I remember well that when I first saw
the movie, in 1983, it astounded and amazed me.

Last night I rented the video and watched it again.

It consists of stunning visual effects combined with
a background of emotionally charged music and chants.
It includes the natural as well as the humanly altered
worlds. Almost everything is speeded up or slowed
down. Its effect is astonishing and provocative. At one
point I felt exhausted, at another languorous.

Viewers may have differing interpretations and
feelings, but I believe most will hold this conviction
in common: It makes you stop and think about "life
out of balance."

It made me stop and think in 1983. It made me
stop and think last night. But what about the years

in between? How long did it take me to forget the lessons I learned and wanted to put into practice when I first saw the film? A year? A month? Probably just a few weeks.

This leads to an urgent question: How can we keep hold of the insights we receive to keep our lives in balance?

What film, play, book, music, or moment of insight has made you stop and think about life out of balance? Go back to it. Review it often. Put it in some place where you'll encounter it often.

For a start, you might rent the *Koyaanisquatsi* video. It will make you stop and think about "life that calls for another way of living."

Today, remember—and review—what has called you to life in balance.

Sitting Still

I have discovered that all human evil comes from this, man's being unable to sit still in a room.

—Blaise Pascal

All human evil? Just what is Pascal trying to say here? If a person, any one of us, were indeed able to sit still in a room, what would that tell us about ourselves that we need to know?

- We are at peace with ourselves. It's hard to imagine someone sitting still and quiet without a degree of inner peace. The sitter would be up in a moment and get busy about many things in order to be distracted from the lack of peace that the sitting identified.

- We have faced our fears. At least the biggest and worst of them. Otherwise they too would be after us, chasing away the calmness and tranquillity that our sitting was about to give us.

- We have perspective and priority. Sitting still in a room allows so much to come up into our consciousness. When we are able to do it, it means that we have been practicing this for a while. It not the first time we've tried it. It means that we have faced the question of what's really important in my life—and what isn't.

- We like our own company. We are with no one but our own self. And we like the company. It implies that we have faced our dark side—our Shadow—and are not surprised by its presence.

A person with these characteristics—a person who is at peace with himself, who has faced her own fears, who has perspective and right priorities in his life, and who likes her own company—just how much evil will such a person cause? Would it not be more likely to find him and her causing joy, creativity, and goodness?

So find a room. Find a chair. See what happens.

Today, sit still in a room for ten minutes.

five

The Spaces in Between

Time-Out

Ah! To do nothing—and to do it well.

—Veronique Vienne

There are many opportunities during times of stress to take a break from the action, a time-out to do nothing. Be on the lookout for them. In the midst of an argument, in the middle of a tense meeting, or as you prepare for a really important interview, take a time-out. This exercise can be an expression of what Veronique Vienne calls doing nothing well.

Simply excuse yourself, momentarily, from the action. Stroll into the next room, wander outside for a moment; it's merely a question of going somewhere else for just a moment. A good bet is the bathroom. No one will deny you and no one will suspect you. It's the perfect way to a time-out.

"Excuse me a moment, Phil, I'll be right back," you say as you knowingly nod and head for the head. Lock the door if you can, and stand in front of the mirror and look at yourself, kindly. Then breathe. Then smile at yourself. Then say what you need to hear: "Keep in mind your ultimate goals here and you'll get through this just fine. Just fine!" Then breathe again. Then return to the stressful meeting with Phil. (It's given him a break too.)

The essence of a time-out, in the bathroom or anywhere, is to get time alone exactly when you need it, in the middle of something stressful.

The stress involved can even be good stress. During a large reception—or holiday celebration, family reunion, or party—we also have need for a moment of stillness, to remember the meaning of the event, to be more awake to its importance.

I can almost guarantee that the outcome will be better with the time-out than without it. The challenge is to remember to do it. And to remember that a time-out is doing nothing well.

Do nothing during several time-outs today. And do it well.

Getting in the Car

Anger is a kind of temporary madness.
—St. Basil (fourth century)

Road rage is a symptom of a temporary madness that is, I believe, a direct result of our overbusy lives. We are simply overwhelmed by all we have to do and therefore we take it out on the drivers who block our way for five seconds. We feel we don't have those five seconds to spare—imagine!—so we are enraged when they are "stolen" from us by another driver.

Road rage is a madness I experience too often, in myself as well as others. So I have devised a special practice for getting in the car.

When you are seated in the car, door closed, seat belt fastened, key in the ignition, ready to go—but before you start the car:

Close your eyes. Take several deep, slow breaths. Sit in silence for a few seconds. Another deep breath. You remember: You want to drive safely, to take account of the weather, the road, the time of day, the amount of traffic, your route. You want to drive defensively and kindly. You are responsible for what you do. You will try to allow others to go where they want to go, rather than fighting them. Those are your choices, your values.

Your first response to a rude driver will be a deep breath and to remember that the act of rudeness is not personal and says nothing about you, and that you don't really know what it says about the other driver.

You note if you are late or if you have sufficient time to arrive at your destination, and if that takes into account the too-frequent traffic jams.

Another deep breath, open your eyes and start the car.

That literally takes a mere fifteen or twenty seconds. But it is not always easy to spend even the seconds. Truth also impels me to say I don't always do it, but when I do, it always helps.

Begin today by trying this getting-into-the-car practice.

Dental Hygiene

Be true to your teeth or your teeth will be false to you.
—dental proverb

All of us have the space-in-between of teeth-brushing. For a moment, bring to mind the times that you brush your teeth. Maybe it's twice a day, in the morning and before bed. If you're really good, it's after every meal. Perhaps occasionally at work.

What are you thinking about as you brush your teeth?

Buddhists remind us, when you brush your teeth, just brush your teeth. Be mindful. Be aware of who you are and what you're doing just now.

My mother's advice, when I was just learning the importance of dental hygiene, was this: "Always brush your teeth for the length of five Hail Marys, and don't rush them."

By my quick calculations, if we spend a minute twice a day—using my mother's Hail Mary standard—by the age of forty we will have already spent about 486 hours, or twenty days, brushing our teeth.

Imagine all those hours filled with intentional mindful breathing, or gentle remembering, or praying, rather than just mindless, impatient scrubbing. Avoid not only false teeth, but also false life.

Beginning today, bring meaning as well as brushing to your dental hygiene.

Grand Central Station

━━━━━━━━━━━━━━━━━━━━━━━━━

In the middle of this famously frenetic public space, I find myself feeling oddly serene.

—David Michaelis

My aunt was fond of saying—I particularly remember her saying it during the family-filled times of Christmas—"It looks like Grand Central Station in here!" She was referring to the hustle and bustle that are the result of the comings and goings of many people in a given place, in this case, our overfull living room.

Grand Central Station in New York has become an American icon of a crowded and busy place, with many people coming and going. Hardly a place for recollection, quietude, or serenity. And yet....

Serenity is available anywhere you seek it.

The author quoted above is a contemporary writer who was researching the recent renovations of the famed rail terminal and it was there, in the middle of that "frenetic public space," that he did feel "oddly serene." Perhaps he added "oddly" because the serenity was so unexpected.

As you find yourself in busy, public places that bustle with activity, let the contrast between what is going on and what you seek, between frenzy and peace, be your guide to serenity. Be still, while all about you swirl the comings and goings of the world.

What are your bustling places? Maybe a transportation terminal, sports stadium, or shopping mall? Or maybe your family room or your kitchen? Wherever they are, let the frenzy call you to the inner serenity that is accessible in any moment.

Identify a frenetic place in your day and find your own odd serenity there.

Wild Places

The wilderness is near as well as dear.
　　　　　　　　—Henry David Thoreau

And, I might add, the nearer, the dearer—at least as far as making the wilderness accessible to as many people as possible. We are used to hearing that the wilderness is dear: "Save the rain forests!" Are we used to hearing that it's often near too?

Those who visit present-day Walden Pond in Concord, Massachusetts, where Thoreau spent his two years in contemplation and solitude, are often struck by how civilized the area has become; it's in the middle of busy communities.

In fact, Walden Pond was not really wilderness even when Thoreau lived there. He writes about visitors, and of hearing wagons on the road, and of going to the village for supplies.

Walden was a wilderness within reach. We have them too: Greenbelts along our rivers, parks in our cities and counties, lake and ocean shores, reservoirs with adjacent park land, trails through woods or forests. All of these are places that can lead us, as Walden did Thoreau, to quietude, to peacefulness, and thus to keeping our priorities clear and our lives on track.

We don't have to trek off to some remote part of the Earth to arrive at the state of wilderness. It is anywhere we come in touch with the peace and beauty of the natural world.

The Sea of Cortez or the community park—the soul can soar in both.

Today identify your close wilderness and make a note to visit soon.

Daily Shower

Cleanliness is next to Godliness.

—proverb

I think some resourceful parent must have invented that saying to shame children into taking a bath, because I've known some less-than-clean folk who seemed well in tune with the divine.

If this saying were indeed and literally true, we would be a very godly nation, for God knows, we're a clean one. And yet, the saying lasts; it must have truth.

However, whether you take a bath or a shower, whether it's in the morning or in the evening, the moments of cleaning oneself are wonderful for a Stillpoint. Most often bathing is a very personal, intimate, and solitary ritual and thus is a natural time to become more awake and call to mind what you need for the day ahead. It might go something like this:

Close your eyes and take some time just to feel the water on your body. Note its temperature, just how it feels. Notice what else you're feeling.

Breathe deeply one, two, three times, slowly.

As your physical energy is aware of the water, at the same time allow your spiritual energy to turn inward. Both movements are part of the same you, and happen in the same moment.

Let the unwelcome effects of the past day wash off your soul just as its physical residue washes off your body.

Let your spirit be refreshed with the cool, clean water of grace just as the warm, clean water brings relaxation and rejuvenation to your body.

You bring to mind those whom you will likely encounter today, and you recall from the past those who would be your models.

Maybe that saying is truer than I thought.

Today, try a Shower Stillpoint.

A Warm Cup of...

Is there anything so welcoming, so promising, so inviting to relaxation as being greeted by, say, a beloved old aunt with the words, "Why, come right in, dear, and I'll fix you a nice cup of tea!" It just seems to say, well, things are not so bad after all.

What is it about taking a cup of warm liquid, whether alone or with someone? It is a quiet and intimate gesture in some ways, and yet one that is allowed almost any time and with almost anyone.

Coffee, tea, chocolate? It makes no difference, although, as Emerson suggests, they do have a different feel to them. "The morning cup of coffee has an exhilaration about it which the cheering influence of the afternoon or evening cup of tea cannot be expected to reproduce." Well, maybe.

Morning or afternoon, coffee or tea, alone or with a friend, taking a warm cup of something calls us to reflect, to remember, perhaps to share.

The next time you're frustrated with work, don't just grin and bear it, take a moment and enjoy a cup of tea. Pay attention to the tea ritual, even if it is only with a tea bag and a paper cup.

When you find yourself discouraged by your slow progress with a project, seize the would-be moment of gloom and treat yourself to a five-minute coffee break. Notice the taste and warmth of the coffee. Pay attention to it. Only then return to your project.

Out of sorts? Feeling cranky? Instead of playing victim, play host or hostess. Invite someone, anyone— the next-door neighbor, the worker in the next cubicle—for a cup of tea.

Today: a warm cup of . . .

Try to Remember

Patience is a virtue. Seersucker is a fabric.
—Bazooka Joe

That was the fortune I recently received in the little comic sheet that came wrapped with my bubble gum. I looked at it for a while, trying to get its meaning. It seemed to mean, Why do we say, "Patience is a virtue" and not say the same about tolerance or thrift, for example? The saying says nothing that you don't already know, just like "Seersucker is a fabric." It also seems to be saying, So what?

But I think I do know why patience is the virtue selected, out of all the virtues, for that simple statement of fact: Because we need to be reminded. Make that, *I* need to be reminded.

The bubble gum came along with the check for my lunch today, a little extra from the restaurant and the waitress, who, to my way of thinking at the time, was about four minutes late in arriving with the check, as she had been with my sandwich. I paid and left quickly, mumbling and grumbling internally about how long I had waited and how inefficient the service was. Then I popped the bubble gum in my mouth and read my fortune.

Oh.

I had a conversation with my wiser self: What was I hurrying to? Nothing. Why didn't I have a wonderful, four-minute Stillpoint instead of becoming unhappy and grouchy? How did I miss such a great occasion to be supportive and friendly to the waitress who was stretched thin at the busy lunch hour?

What are your moments of frustration and impatience? Join me in making an effort—next time!—to be awake enough at those moments to turn them into moments of life.

If you're in a tight spot today, try to breathe and remember what's important.

Flying

Oh! I have slipped the surly bonds of Earth...
and touched the face of God.

—John G. Magee, Jr.

These are the first and last lines of a remarkable poem, "High Flight," written on the back of a letter to his parents by a pilot in the Royal Canadian Air Force who perished in World War II.

It is a reminder that flying is the perfect time for reflection:

The exhilaration of speeding down the runway to take-off and soaring into flight! It's an occasion that can always cause you wonder.

From up here you have a totally different perspective. What seemed to be important a while ago now, from this point of view, seems less so. Other parts of life loom larger and more urgent.

At 30,000 feet and 600 miles an hour, you feel on the edge of the universe. Almost a space traveler. God seems closer.

Flying indeed is the perfect time to come back to ourselves. In fact, it's hard to image a better opportunity. And the metaphors and imagery suggested by flying support a poetic and spiritual moment.

The next time you're in flight, before you take out the laptop, before you reach for the cell phone, before you open your book, look out the window or into your soul, or both.

You too just might touch the face of God.

The next time you fly, or see a plane flying, reflect....

La Bella Luna

RONNIE: What's the matter?

LORETTA: Nothing, I'm looking at the moon. I never seen a moon like that before.

RONNIE: Makes you look like an angel.

—from *Moonstruck*

If there is one symbol that more than any other calls human beings to a moment of stillness and reflection, it must be the moon.

Which of us cannot identify many moments in our lives when we noticed the moon, made a comment on its particular way of being out this night, and thus brought ourselves, and perhaps those with us, to a moment of transcendence?

Moonstruck is a happy movie about an Italian family in Brooklyn. The beautiful moon, *la bella luna,* is a symbol that runs through the story and calls each of the main characters to a moment of quiet reflection, and thus to a deeper recognition of their love.

The above dialogue is between Loretta (played by Cher) and Ronnie (Nicholas Cage) and is a moment of recognition for them.

Everyone in the film has pain and hurt with which they struggle, sometimes without a lot of success. The moon is the silent witness to all of their lives. The moon seems to say, by its simple and mysterious presence, that there is more to life than sometimes it seems, there are some people you can indeed trust, and it's important to follow your heart.

But first you have to notice it. You have to spend some time looking at the moon—or perhaps howling at it—in order for it to call you to a moment of reflection and insight.

Anticipate your next encounter with *la bella luna*. Determine to allow it to bring you to a moment of quiet contemplation.

Tonight, look for the moon.

Still Time

Time can stand still, I am convinced of it; something snags and stops, turning and turning, like a leaf on a stream.

−John Banville

Yes, I am also convinced that time can stand still. I believe, in fact, that this stopped time is the most real time of all. The Irish writer John Banville, in his novel *The Untouchable,* describes the desire of one of his characters to tell his listener about the really "true things":

"I wanted to tell her about the blade of sunlight cleaving to the velvet shadows . . . of the incongruous gaiety of the rain shower that fell the day of my father's funeral, of that night . . . when I saw the red ship under the Blackfriars Bridge and conceived of the tragic significance of my life: in other words, the real things; the true things."

These are the moments when time stands still. Sunlight, a rain shower, and a red ship are symbols that carry meaning. But Banville's character's heart holds "the real things." His inner life was more urgently meaningful than the externals about which he will actually speak: why he was in the sunlight at that moment, with whom he was walking when he saw the red ship, even his father's funeral.

When time stands still, you can be sure that something very important is leaping in.

To allow this pregnant calm, we must be still, like a leaf slowly turning and turning on a stream, caught in an eddy, while the stream continues its fall to the sea.

Watch for your time-standing-still moments as you go about your busy days. What are they like for you? Can you recall some from your past?

And especially, watch for the truth. Pay a lot of attention to the truth that leaps in at those moments, for it will surely enrich your life.

What will help you notice time standing still?

A Living Picture

A picture lives by companionship. It dies by the same token. It is therefore risky to send it out into the world. How often it must be impaired by the eyes of the unfeeling.

—Mark Rothko

Do you feel the full impact of that statement? It is really quite a remarkable thing to say. A picture *lives* by companionship? Unfeeling eyes can hurt it? These are words of one who lives in the world of paradox and mystery, below the surface, in the spirit world, the most real and certainly the most interesting of all the worlds.

One of my deep convictions is that we need to pay more attention to artists. They reflect and interpret our world. They see what the rest of us are too busy, too distracted, or otherwise incapable of seeing. They say to us simply: Look at this! Take some time and see this! It's important!

Too often we dismiss artists as temperamental and difficult and even as unwilling to get a "real" job.

Except for the very few who become trendy and collectable in their lifetimes, most die poor. The great ones make money for heirs and collectors.

It is not surprising that the words above come from the twentieth-century painter, Mark Rothko. Born in Russia, he lived and worked in America. He is a color-field painter of the abstract expressionist school. His late and most recognized works are huge canvases of softly painted or blurred blocks of color, often dark, which seem to float in front of another colored ground. If you stand quietly before one in a museum long enough, you will probably hear some comments which indicate that the art is challenging to the viewer. Some words might be statements of the "unfeeling" that can "impair" the work.

I'm not sure I understand or even appreciate Rothko's work, but I try to remember his words so as not to hurt his picture with my eyes.

Next time you visit a museum, be aware of your power.

Traveling

Traveling is glamorous only in retrospect.
—Paul Theroux

And sometimes not even in retrospect! I wonder when traveling stopped being fun and became ... what? Challenging! Especially if it involves air travel. And the challenge increases when you are traveling for work and have a tight schedule or when you are traveling with children.

It seems, no matter our efforts to the contrary, that all travel is hurried.

So how can we transform a terrible trip into a serene journey? Well, for starters, we acknowledge what we cannot control: the airlines, the availability of a taxi, the arrival time of the train, where our baggage ends up, and the weather.

But here are a few things we can do:

Most important, expect challenges during any journey and prepare yourself mentally to accept and deal with them as a normal part of travel.

Allow more time between when you leave and when you have to be there. This is a difficult one—and sometime we just can't do it. Do it when you can. Add an afternoon or a day as buffer time when you can. If you don't need it, great! You've found some time for yourself.

Generously place quiet moments in your traveling time. These traveling Stillpoints might focus on your journey's purpose, stretching and remembering, or mentally rehearsing how you want to feel when you arrive. If your travel allows time to read, these quiet moments could be connected to what you're reading. How we travel is how we'll arrive.

Think of the journey not as a means to an end—merely a way to get somewhere else—but a reality with its own life and identity. Frequently call to mind the Taoist saying, "The journey is the reward."

Resolve today: My next trip can be a more peaceful journey.

six

Creating Opportunities for Serenity

Writing

Learn as much by writing as by reading.
—Lord Acton

By its nature, writing slows you down. With pencil and pad relaxing on your sofa, or with laptop at 30,000 feet and supersonic speed, writing focuses your attention, stills your soul.

But is it, as the learned lord suggests, a way to learn? If so, what can be learned from writing? I can't answer for Lord Acton, but I know some of the ways it works for me.

When I write, I must go more deeply in search and exploration of myself. Thus I learn, more than anything, about me.

When I write, I must continually research the material. Thus I learn about the world.

When I write, I pursue the appropriate word to use, with the precise meaning I need. I want to find the exact brocard, craft the precise zeugma.

When you write in a diary or in a journal, who knows what will pop out of your pen? Sometimes you don't realize what you have written until, perhaps months later, you return to read it. *I wrote that?*

Write poetry. It allows you to express feelings and ideas that otherwise might not have been born. Refine and revise your poems until they are most pleasing to you. No need to worry about publication.

Write letters. Especially these days, a handwritten letter says that you took extra time and special effort. Write e-mails. Write postcards to friends. Write notes to yourself.

Write stories. Write essays. As you let the world hear from you, you'll probably hear from the world in some way.

Write anything, and learn much.

Determine to spend time today writing something.

The Singer, Not the Song

Even if you can't sing well, sing. Sing to yourself. Sing in the privacy of your own home. But sing.

—Rebbe Nachman

Why does the spiritual teacher encourage us to sing?

Isn't it because there is nothing quite so effective as singing to get what is inside of you out? Nothing better expresses your feelings and attitudes to the world, whether or not any of the world is hearing it.

The point is not the hearing; it's the singing.

Singing creates a habit of moving inner feelings to accessibility, to a place where other people can share them. And in order to move them out, you have to encounter them, forge them into words and melody, and send them forth in all their harmony and beauty. Or in all their off-key cacophony. No matter.

When we are awake to the moment, when we are aware of ourselves, when we remember who we are, we will sing: a melancholy ballad, a soaring saraband, or a droning dirge; it depends on what is inside. Sing in the shower as you prepare for the day, in the car as you drive home from work, during your morning walk. Sing to your children, or with them.

One of the reasons I love musicals—that most American expression of theater—is the way the characters, in an unselfconscious and unlikely way, burst out into song at all the right moments. Maybe we all would love the freedom to do that.

Sometime today: Stop and sing! Out loud!

Books

I cannot live without books.

—Thomas Jefferson

That's a statement of a person with a passion. It's easy to understand not being able to live without food or water or even companionship, but books? Yes, books!

Oh, Jefferson would no doubt have continued to live without them, he probably wouldn't really have died, but neither would he have been as fully alive as he wanted to be.

Of the many gifts of the world that can lead us to contemplation, to creative reverie, to quiet moments of being in the present, perhaps books are the most powerful. Or am I just revealing my own biased attraction to Jefferson's words?

My father used to love to say to someone who had just given him a book as a gift, "Oh, that's too bad, I already have a book!" as if it were a duplicate of a necktie.

His humor got at a deeper truth: you really can't have too many books. They hold the world for our perusal.

I have a list of special books. Currently it contains five titles. I call it my life-changing book list. Each of these volumes has undeniably changed the way I live. The first title on the list is *Stuart Little* by E. B. White. In truth, the list could contain all the books I have ever read, for they have all changed my life in some way.

What are some significant books in your life?

Imagine yourself with one of them, seated in your favorite chair, the book held loosely in your lap, staring into space in contemplation of something the writer has just suggested to you, and which you are now following in your own reverie....

Spend some time with a favorite book today.

A Place at Home

People are feeling a need to sit still, to breathe, to take a pause in their daily routine.

–from *Metropolitan Home* magazine

This is from *Metropolitan Home?* Yes, it appears in an introduction to one of their home-of-the-month articles, which features a meditation room designed on the ancient principles of feng shui, the Chinese art of arranging things in your home based on spiritual principles.

It's another example of how desperately we all need to find serenity in our lives. "And this need for reflection, for quality down-time," say the editors, "applies equally to living rooms and bedrooms, kitchens and baths. People have long been devoted to their homes; what we have begun to see are homes that are themselves devotional."

We all have need for sacred space. Churches and synagogues and mosques are sacred spaces for many people. And certainly a place for quiet moments or for meditation is not new to many homes, although most will not have a separate room dedicated exclusively to that purpose as does the magazine's featured home.

In many cultures, homes have what might be described as a shrine, or a devotional place with meaningful sacred symbols.

My own shrine is simply the corner of a bookshelf. It holds symbols of life for me. Among them are nails from a torn-down building, a family medal, a Costa Rican cross, and a replica of a Haida totem.

Think of your own home. Is there a place there that calls you, and those with whom you live, to be still, to be quiet? Having such a space is important, for when you go there, you are immediately surrounded by a feeling that you want to go in.

If there is a devotional place in your home,
enjoy it today. If not, would you create one?

The Sentences

*... and the passerby, should he turn round to make sure
that I have not gone astray, may be amazed to see me
still standing there ... gazing at the steeple for hours on
end....*

—Marcel Proust

About a year ago, I decided that my exposure to the
great works of world literature was too limited,
so I began to go back, so to speak, and catch up. Why
I decided to begin with Proust, the French novelist,
is anyone's guess.

But that's where I began, and that's where I am
still, creeping my way through *Swann's Way,* the first
of the seven volumes of his epic novel *Remembrance
of Things Past.*

The creeping is not because it is dull, which it rarely
is, although it can be slow moving; nor is it because
the writing is complex; that too is characteristic. It is
because of the sentences. Oh, the sentences!

I have never read such sentences. They can go on
forever and ever, sometimes taking up the whole page.

And they contain entire worlds of feeling, and nuanced insights into human behavior, and observation of life. So I read them over and over. That's why I'm creeping. It just takes me a long time to read, and then re-read, all those improbable sentences.

The snippet quoted above is from one of them, one of my favorites. It is fully half a page long, and it describes not something that happened in his life, but something that might have happened, had a few other things occurred as well.

Why, I ask myself, do I read these boulderlike sentences over and over again?

I read them over and over because they make me still. At least that's one of their effects. There are others.

Think of some reading that makes you still, centered, or quiet. Take it from the shelf today.

A Walking Solution

Solvitur ambulando.

—St. Jerome

The literal translation of St. Jerome's Latin words is, "It is solved walking." In other words, if you have a problem to solve—or a decision to make, or a crisis to face, or a knotty question to resolve—take a walk. Take a walk? Yes.

Jerome must have had many problems to solve. He is known for translating the entire Bible from its original languages into Latin. And he must have known this walking-around wisdom from firsthand experience. He would return to his writing table refreshed from his walk, able now to render a sentence that had resisted his previous efforts, into the smooth-flowing language that is the hallmark of his translation.

In many ways, the fourth-century challenges of Jerome are probably not much different—at least in their type, if not in their frequency—from the twenty-first century problems we face today.

Walking solves problems because it allows the soul-part to rest while the body-part works. It allows the mind to notice the air, the light, and what's going on in the village. These processes refresh the intellect and allow it to cut through what formerly had been too tough a surface.

This working-it-out, this clearing and refreshing, are processes that happen on their own, during the walk. You don't have to bring your problem-to-be-solved with you on the walk. If you do, it might not work. Rather, leave the problems behind. Then go for a walk.

This is an all-win proposition: It's enjoyable, it's refreshing, it's a way to solve problems, and it's free.

Got a problem to solve? Leave it and take a walk.

Still Hunting

---

*I think that I could turn and live with the animals, they
are so placid and self-contained.*

—Walt Whitman

A book I have enjoyed for several years is *Listening
to Nature* by Joseph Cornell. In it he describes
many ways to deepen your awareness of nature. One
way he tells about was originated by American Indians.
It's about hunting, but it has noting to do with stalk-
ing and killing animals. It is called still hunting.

It involves first entering the world of nature, a
woods, a desert, a forest, a place where there are wild
animals of any kind, small or large. Your entrance there
in some way will disturb the animals' natural activity,
so the idea is to sit as still as possible in that place
"waiting for the world of nature to return to its
normal, harmonious routine."

You choose a place where your profile is somewhat
hidden by shadows, leaves, or bushes, or broken up by
trees or rocks. You melt into the landscape and allow
nature to come back to its normal life around you.

You approach the place quietly, wear clothes that blend in with your surroundings, breathe quietly, eyes open and observing, ears alert for the small changes. "Sit for at least twenty minutes," Cornell advises.

"Your experience will be most enjoyable if you free your mind from expectations. Don't expect a caravan of animals to come parading by."

Just pay "attention to what you do see and hear: busy insects, singing birds, and breezes bringing the trees to life."

Could you imagine the possibility of teaching still hunting to a young person? It might be a way to balance their hours in the video arcade.

Make plans for a still hunting expedition. Maybe invite some kids.

Nature as Therapist

✦————————————————✦

*There is nothing so good as the wind and the sun for
driving the foolishness out of one.*

—Roycroft Epigrams, 1923

Afellow psychotherapist and I have often joked
that when the weather turns warm and balmy
in the spring, we seem to have fewer new clients and
more appointment cancellations, whereas the cold
and dark months of winter bring a greater number of
ardent seekers to our doors.

Nature indeed is a good therapist. So make an
appointment with what drives the foolishness out
of you.

Is it the wind blowing strong in your face as you
stand on the ocean shore or mountaintop, cleaning
out, as it were, the old, gathered cobwebs of pain or
sadness?

The sun? It warms your back as you take a walk
in the morning, inviting you into the day, and assur-
ing you that all is right in the heavens.

The rain? In spritzes or in torrents, it brings life to
our Earth, food to our tables, and a feeling of closeness

and security when seen through the window of a dry and warm home.

Clouds? Always changing and moving and sometimes totally absent or represented by the merest waft, they are always taking the shapes of things or reminding us of something. And they never fail to uplift the spirit.

And Nature is almost always accessible. In cities and office buildings look for plants and indoor trees to spend a moment with, windows with views of the sky, a nearby city park or greenbelt where you can pause and refresh, drive out the foolishness, and return to life.

Today, make an appointment for a therapy session with Nature.

Uncommon Hours

*If one advances confidently in the direction of his
dreams, and endeavors to live a life which he has
imagined, he will meet with a success unexpected in
common hours.*

—Henry David Thoreau

Three things strike me about these words of
Thoreau:

First, I'm drawn to Thoreau's phrase "common hours,"
especially as it implies the presence of uncommon
hours. What are those uncommon hours?

Second, I note the sexist language. Please don't dismiss this as an insignificant problem, or only the concern of outspoken feminists. Language is immensely
important and tells us—for the most part subliminally—how we are to treat others in our world. We
live our language; our language creates our realities.

But Thoreau lived in another era (the mid-nineteenth century) so we can't fairly judge him by our
standards. But what am I, writing now, to do with his
language? Do I insert "or she" after every "he"? Do

I call attention to it (as I am now, but normally don't)? Or do I just let it pass? None of the answers satisfies. I will bring the problem to my uncommon hours.

Third, I notice he says the imagination is somehow a key in bringing something practically into your life. To achieve something in practice, you must first imagine it.

Years ago, I mentioned to a writer friend, "I can't imagine writing a novel." To which she replied, "Then, of course, you can't." Oh. Of course. Another topic for my uncommon hours.

Seek out your uncommon hours with determination! You will find them among your days, weeks, months, and years. In those hours you will dream of possibilities, create wondrous realities, ponder the thorny problems of life, and imagine what only you can imagine!

Will you find an uncommon hour today?
Why not?

Monastics

'Tis not the habit that makes the monk.
—Thomas Fuller

Monasteries and convents are where men and women go to be monastics, to live the quiet life of prayer, simplicity, and work in a community of the like-minded.

But many men and women who live in the larger world, with relationships, families, careers, and friends, are successful in bringing parts of the monastic life into their secular routines.

Dennis is a professional health care provider, with a spouse and a full life of patients and teaching. But he also finds time for meditation, a daily horarium of prayer, and several spaces of quiet contemplation. He used to be a monk in a monastery; now he's a "monk" in his home and office.

Patricia is a nurse. She leads a very quiet but full life of service, working at the hospital, and volunteering much time to community projects that serve children. Her day is built upon a structure of prayer and quietude. This is her life of choice. Her husband, of a similar inclination, often joins her.

Lisa is an artist. She spends most of her day in her studio painting, which for her is a spiritual practice. She lives alone and has an active social life with family members, friends, and colleagues.

It is clear that the people mentioned here have made the monastic part of their lives a priority and thus have chosen to forgo other aspects. Most of us are not in a position to make such a choice. Two of those described above are parents but none have children living at home.

Even if your circumstances are different, is there a way, even a small way, you would like to express the monastic hidden in you?

Today, reflect on the possibility of monastic moments.

A New Place

My favorite thing is to go where I've never been.
—Diane Arbus

We've all heard stories of women and men who, after a long life of apparent contentment—say, marriage and family or a longtime career—decide suddenly to leave it all. They quit their jobs, divorce their spouses, leave the kids, and leap. The outcomes of the leap vary from bliss to disaster, but one thing remains constant: the pain they leave behind.

What happens to these people? Why do some do it while for others the possibility never occurs? I have no answers, but I have a suspicion that it has to do with a lack of diversity and newness.

Years ago I knew a woman who was married to a mean-hearted and violent man, a closet alcoholic, who grossly mistreated her and their five children. They were poor and lived in deep, quiet terror. Nothing changed for years. Even though encouraged by others to escape her cruel life, she remained steadfastly loyal to her vows, dogged to her obligations.

Then one day she died. No warning, no identifiable illness.

There was never anything new in her life. Always the same, and most of it painful. No possibility of going where she'd never been. Her leap was into death. I'm convinced she died from a broken spirit.

She was, I'm sure, convinced that she was doing the right thing, the moral thing. She was staying the course. In a way she was a hidden saint.

But the pain she left behind? The pain that her children are surely carrying yet today? That's what I noticed.

The story encourages me, and I hope you, to go where you've never been, in an airplane or in your spirit, alone or with someone. Go to a new place where you'd love to be, and keep going to new places. A gradual leap leaves less pain.

Today, take some quiet time to plan your trip to a place where you've never been.

Keeping the Sabbath

The Sabbath was made for man, not man for the Sabbath.

–Luke 4:2

Where did the day of rest go? Whether your religious tradition observes Saturday (the original Sabbath) or Sunday, or even if in your tradition there is no day of rest at all, we all need a Sabbath. We all need a day of rest—not a day of shopping, catching up on work, or running all over the place on errands. A day of rest, a day of doing nothing.

A recent Sunday newspaper comic strip, Greg Howard's *Sally Forth,* featured an agenda for Sundays:

THINGS TO DO ON SUNDAY

Have a cup of tea.

Gaze into the distance.

Read the paper.

Stretch.

Have another cup of tea.

The essence of the traditional Sabbath is to celebrate one's spiritual practice and to rest from work.

For some, work in the yard or garden is not really work, but pleasure.

For others, an outing with the family or friends is a way to rest.

However, if you're like me, you hear yourself saying, "Fine, but when am I supposed to get the chores done?" Sometimes you have to settle for a partial Sabbath. Find a chore you can skip this week and take a couple of hours on Sunday morning with coffee and the newspaper or a Saturday afternoon's long walk in the park.

This week inaugurate or rejuvenate your Sabbath observance. Remember: No work, for at least part of the day.

Staying Home

There is nothing like staying home for real comfort.

—Jane Austen

Some reflections on staying home:

Home alone! I feel lucky when I have my home to myself for a while.

"A place you don't have to deserve." That's how poet Robert Frost refers to home.

It seems to me a feeling of safety should exist in my home. I shouldn't have to be vigilant there.

Some questions about staying home:

Do you have real comfort in your home? How can you make your home more inviting for you to stay there more often? Paint the walls a new color? Find a comfortable, well- lighted place to read? Is there the degree of order and neatness you need?

No time alone? See if you can come up with times when no one else is around, early in the morning maybe.

No space to separate from spouse, kids, housemates? Can you designate a room as a place apart where one can go and be allowed to be alone?

What will I do if I just stay home? Fuss around. Look through drawers. Write a letter or two. Browse books. Bake a cake. Take a walk. Balance the checkbook. Make a phone call. Read a poem. Write a poem. Sit still.

Yes, there is a lot to do out there, many cultural attractions, or many naturally beautiful places to visit. They'll always be there, or others like them, or better ones.

But it's Saturday night and everyone is out having fun!

Yes, and you are staying home and having fun.

Today, make plans to stay home for real comfort.

You've Gotta Have Art!

To give a list of the great artists that the world has seen would be to name a list of lovers.

—Roycroft Epigrams, 1923

I f everyday serenity were to have a patron artist, I am aware of none more suitable than Jan Vermeer, a Dutch painter who lived and worked in Delft in the mid-seventeenth century. "Vermeer's genius was in probing those moments when one feels alone and immersed in one's thoughts," notes art historian A. K. Wheelock.

Perhaps you recall seeing his well-known *Young Woman with a Water Jug.* It portrays a woman—she wears a nunlike head and shoulder covering—one hand on a water pitcher, the other reaching toward a window, which casts light and shadow upon her as she gazes into mid-space. The artist captures her in this moment of reflection, of contemplation.

Many of Vermeer's paintings capture individuals, mostly women, most often in the light of a window, in these moments of reverie, of dream-like trance, of contemplation.

The *Young Woman,* like all of Vermeer's paintings, makes it easy to know that he tendered a deep love for the part of the world he painted. And it gets me wondering...

What is the woman pondering? What has captured her inner attention so? Has she thought of someone? A memory? There's a slight smile on her face; is she in a light mood, about to laugh? Or is she just pausing, enjoying the peace of the moment?...until I too am still.

What art speaks to you of deep love of the world? Brings you to a moment of quiet contemplation?

Today find a work of art that leads you to stillness, to contemplation.

The Luxury of Solitude

The only true time which man can properly call his own [is] that which he has all to himself; the rest...is other people's time.

—Charles Lamb

Let's say you have a particularly hard week coming up, a week overfilled with difficult and demanding challenges. You get tired just thinking about it. This is the time to plan ahead for a luxurious time of solitude for yourself.

To balance your life, when you are finished with living on other people's time, you need to plan a time of your own, a time of solitude and peace.

Planning ahead brings a unique benefit: As you plan and contemplate your time alone, you bring some of that energy to the present moment and thus feel a bit more relaxed right now.

As you go about meeting the challenges of the week—in the middle of a tense meeting, at a consultation with the doctor, while negotiating a difficult contract, while traveling to a confrontational encounter—you can remember that soon you will leave all this behind.

Later, when you have basked in your time of solitude, you will be more capable of again being with people and facing a demanding week in a more fulfilling way.

After solitude, your presence in society will be more authentic.

Today, plan a time of solitude.

Trees

I go among trees and sit still.

—Wendell Berry

Is there a better place than among trees to sit still? They seem to foster stillness, quietude, and reverie. Think of the trees you have known, specific ones that you remember from past times and places, or those in your life now, perhaps right outside your window. Reflect on them for a moment....

Here are snippets from my reverie:

In the backyard of my childhood home in Ohio was a flowering plum with dark red leaves and rough, dark-gray bark, growing next to the garage. I would run toward it at breakneck speed, grab onto its lowest limb, swing up to the next, then up to the next, now bracing my foot on an awkwardly protruding branch which had a little give to it, which would push me to the last limb and thus to my destination, the "porch" on top of the garage. The journey was one flowing movement, ground to roof, the plum tree the vehicle. We ate the plums too. The flowering plum outside my window now looks nothing like the other one, but it reminds me....

Two giant...were they oaks? maples? Grew so close together that my grandfather put up a swing between them with long ropes stretching far up the towering trunks. We would swing for hours....

It was a delicate palm tree, just the right size. We saw it beside the road in Cali, Colombia, and quickly agreed with the owner on a price. We dug it up and took it home and planted it in the living room, which was, in that climate, partially open to the sky. The little palm thrived, contrary to all predictions. I wonder, is it still there...?

Trees can make you still; stillness can bring memories...climbing, swinging, planting....

Allow the trees in your life—past and present— to lead you to reverie.

seven

Defining
Your Values

Covering the Bases

If I die, I forgive you; if I recover, we'll see.
—Spanish proverb

I always wonder how some people know exactly what virtue is and how to live it. It seems to me that just when you seem to get it down, it changes. Today kindness leads me to treat someone with confrontation, tomorrow with care. What, indeed, is kindness? Rather would I say that she is a kind person; his was a kind act.

And so often what might seem virtuous to me, some act of justice or charity or honesty, in reality is an act that gets me what I want; I'm simply covering all the bases.

Consider the wry saying above. The point seems to be that, live or die, I have not forgiven you. Not really. Forgiveness with a condition, in this case my death, is not forgiveness. Even so, the words have an appealing human touch to them. We can relate to them.

Emerson even speaks of virtues that don't appear to be virtues: "The virtues of society are the vices of the saint."

So, all said and done, how can we know what virtue is and what it isn't? How do we know that we have not placed a convenient condition on our virtue—a condition that will only pop into view when it's needed ("if I recover. . .")?

Here are a couple suggestions for ways to start the process: To know virtue and true goodness, withdraw from the marketplace and know your own heart as deeply as you can. To withhold hasty and unfair judgment on others, walk a few miles, quietly in your mind, in their moccasins.

When you return to the marketplace, chances are better that you will arrive with an intuitive recognition of virtuous acts, or their absence, in you and in others.

Reflect on true virtue today, in yourself, in others.

The Things of the World

My soul can find no staircase to heaven unless it be through earth's loveliness.

—Michelangelo

I certainly appreciate the great artist's words. The German poet Rainer Maria Rilke frequently refers to "the things of the world" with the same attitude of appreciation, enjoyment, and transcendence.

Although I am somewhat embarrassed to admit it, I love "things." I recall twice in my life when this was pointed out to me.

Years ago, I lived and worked in Cali, Colombia. During a visit to our parish center, the local bishop looked around my room and commented, to my surprise, "You really enjoy lots of little things *[cositas]*, don't you?"

When my brother and sister-in-law visited me years later in California, she said, "I've never seen a home with so many little things!"

My first response in both cases was to feel defensive. After all, I have interest in life directions that emphasize the spiritual, not the material dimensions. So why so many things?

Michelangelo to my rescue. Why separate the things of the world from spirituality? Away with the too prevalent separation of the physical and the spiritual! A piece of art, a well-turned pot, a finely wrought chair? These are Earth's loveliness. They can lead to heaven.

But the connection is easy to forget. One can begin to amass many things just for their own sake, or merely for the sake of having more and more of them.

That's where Stopping comes into the picture. It helps you to keep perspective, to know that things in themselves have no enduring value or importance, that generosity is more important than accumulation.

Today take time to consider your things and your attitude toward them.

Living Spiritually

It is when you are really living in the present . . . that you
are living spiritually.

—Brenda Ueland

S*piritual* is a difficult word, and for that reason,
many people avoid it. Jon Kabat-Zinn's comments are a good expression of this attitude: "As much
as I can, I avoid using the word *spiritual* altogether,"
he says. "I find it neither useful nor necessary nor
appropriate. . . . I have a problem with the inaccurate,
incomplete, and frequently misguided connotations
of [the] word."

I respect this attitude and, for a while, espoused it.
But most people continue to use the words *spiritual*
and *spirituality,* and I cannot find others that take their
place more effectively. So I (somewhat arbitrarily)
assign meaning to the words and thus have come to
appreciate and value them.

The meaning of *spirituality* that I choose to
embrace—for it is not only my definition—is: the
meanings and values by which you live your life,

combined with, for believers, the way you experience the divine. The combination of God, meanings, and values is spirituality.

But, of course, this does not exhaust the ways to define it, or indeed the ways to experience it (thus the value of the doubters).

I'm drawn to Brenda Ueland's expression above. The whole quote is: "It is when you are really living in the present—working, thinking, lost, absorbed in something you care about very much, that you are living spiritually." I like that very much. Michelangelo expressed it this way: "It is well with me only when I have a chisel in my hand."

It is exactly during those moments, when your meanings and your values and your awareness of God combine to create the energy that takes charge of your time, that you live life to the fullest.

Identify the ways your spirituality is expressed throughout the day.

In the Next Seat

Are you looking for me? I am in the next seat.
My shoulder is against yours.

–Kabir

That's not the guy sitting next to you on the subway speaking; it's God. Poets seem to talk for God a lot. Well, I suppose someone has to do it. This poet is a Sufi Muslim who was born in the mid-1400s.

I wonder why it is so easy to forget the immanence of God? It is clearly proposed by the world's religions: God dwells within each of us. But we forget.

Nothing better than to allow the whole poem (in Robert Bly's translation) to speak to us:

Are you looking for me? I am in the next seat.
My shoulder is against yours.
You will not find me in stupas, nor in Indian shrine
    rooms, nor in the synagogue, nor in cathedrals:
not in masses, nor kirtans, not in legs winding around
    your own neck, nor in eating nothing but vegetables.
When you really look for me, you will see me
    instantly—

you will find me in the tiniest house of time.
Kabir says, "Student, tell me, what is God?
He is the breath inside the breath."

Be still, wake up! I say to myself. Stop running all over the place and just look into the eyes gazing upon you from the next seat.

Today, notice the loving gaze upon you from the next seat.

Bigger: Better or Worse?

In a small house God has his corner, in a big house he has to stand in the hall.

—Swedish proverb

The more I give power to the idea that bigger is always better, the more I push out the presence of the smaller, quieter, often spiritual realities that call me to my values.

The more material resources at my disposal, the more difficult it is to acknowledge my lack of control in life, my responsibility in being part of the human community. The more distractions I allow, the less will I notice my chosen spiritual values.

A big house is not a bad thing and a small house is not a good thing. They are just things to be reckoned with, things to be named as powers capable of influencing whether God and spiritual values are in the place you want them.

Many of us live—especially compared to the rest of the world's population—in big houses, meaning we have a having a good number of possessions and resources.

Perhaps this is the reason for the popularity of the idea of simplicity and simple living. Perhaps we are connecting thoughtless accumulation of things with a frustrating—and often fast—life, and simplicity with peace and slowing down.

It is challenging but certainly possible to have a big house with your spiritual priorities in their proper corner. It is also possible to have a small house and God, hat in hand, standing in the hall.

What is the size of your house? Where are your spiritual values?

Today, consciously bring to mind the size of your house and then notice where God is in it.

The Friend of Silence

[God] cannot be found in noise and restlessness. God is the friend of silence.

—Mother Teresa of Calcutta

For Mother Teresa, activity did not lead to God, silence did.

The point to consider is what leads you to an attitude of prayer, to making contact with the divine?

Here are some questions to ponder:

What kind of silence speaks to you of God? There are many kinds of silences. I can imagine that for some, perhaps for you, the roar of the ocean or even the hum of urban noise is a kind of silence that can lead to God. Is it the silence that comes from the tumult of a storm? From the roar of the surf? Or do you prefer the deeper quiet of a forest glade?

Who encourages you to an attitude of silence or prayer? A friend? A saint, officially canonized or not?

Where do you feel most quiet or most open to the divine? At home? In a church? Perhaps a museum or a park?

What are some personal links to prayer? A book or image? A place? Sacred texts?

For Mother Teresa, activity did not lead to God, silence did; but it is also obvious that the God she encountered in silence led her to remarkable activity.

This is a fine example of the truth that the reason for Stopping is going. Spending time doing nothing creatively and on purpose, giving your spiritual values opportunity to be present and urgent to you, has the result of prioritizing your whole life. It clarifies and motivates. It can move you to magnificent activity.

Today, find some silence in which to spend some moments.

Care

---

*Life is not lost by dying; life is lost minute by minute,
day by dragging day, in all the small uncaring ways.*
—Stephen Vincent Benét

One of the best ways, it seems to me, to determine your spirituality—the meanings and values by which you live—is to ask yourself the question, What do I really care about?

Recently I took some shirts to the laundry, as I do quite regularly. It is a family-run business and over the years I have come to know the family members who work there. This time I noticed a couple of my shirts had buttons missing. The woman who owns the laundry noticed the missing buttons too and offered to replace them. "Wonderful," I said, "Yes, please do."

A week later, when I went to pick up my shirts, I noticed that she had indeed carefully replaced the buttons—matching them exactly—but was not charging me for the work. I called it to her attention. "Oh, no," she said, "I am happy to do it for you."

Her single act of caring made me notice, in that moment, something else about her. She was caring in everything she did: her gestures, her words, her work, her sewing, her counting of the shirts, her handing me the package, her smile, her making change.

I noticed too, from my many brief visits, that she also cared about friendly, competent service, doing more than she was paid to do, being generous, her family.

She is not missing life. "In all the small...ways," she cares.

Look for all your small ways to care today and for the expression of care by others.

Awesome

Awe is the finest portion of mankind. . . . In awe one feels profoundly the immense.

—Goethe

"Awesome!" may be the way your teenager responds to what has just pleased her greatly, be it a motorcycle ride, the film she just saw, or even a chocolate chip cookie. (At least, I think they're still using the word.) Even though I sometimes envy teenagers' ability to be amazed by the simple pleasures life has to offer, I prefer Goethe's definition of the word and like to save it for a more deserving occasion.

It is the finest portion we have. Awe is not just an expression of wonder and reverence and respect. In awe, these feelings are mingled with dread or fear, and in its embrace we are aware of the presence of the immense.

The feeling of awe is a sign that we have a certain degree of being awake, aware, and open to the combination of feelings that create it. When we are in its embrace, we tend to be still, silent, observant. Awe is often anticipated and fostered when we are alone and at rest. When awestruck in the presence of other people, each will spend that moment of awe alone, absorbed, riveted by the power. Only later will we share the experience as we reflect on it.

"Make this Bed with Awe—" are the poetic words Emily Dickinson used as she anticipated her death. A deathbed is indeed to be made with awe, for in it we await the immense and "excellent and fair" judgment. What are some other moments when *awesome* is the right word for you? As I think again, I am wondering about the teenager's chocolate chip cookie and motorcycle ride. Could those really be awesome?

To what do you truly respond, "Awesome!"

Glitz

The most successful performer is not the person with the truth but the one with the sharpest tongue and the handiest numbers.

—Mark Kingwell

I agree with Kingwell's statement. I wonder if it has always been true. My guess is that even if it has been true to some extent, it is truer now, more widespread. This statement is from an article in *Harper's* magazine; he is speaking specifically of guests on talk shows.

In my professional speaking association, a popular concept is "infotainment," implying that people still want some good, solid information, but you'll only get it across if you entertain them.

What about people with the important truths who are not entertaining? I can recall several teachers in that category; I had to make an effort to learn from them. Isn't there a qualitative difference in the learning experience? Don't careful listening, experiment, and discovery lead to a different form of knowledge than that gained through "infotainment"? Thus we need to pay attention to what Kingwell calls "those unadorned truths that take effort to achieve." Certainly the best of all worlds is to present truth in an entertaining way. But how often do we get the best of all worlds? And thus how much of the truth do we miss?

I'm beginning to think—I hope it's not a permanent case of cynicism setting in—that the more glitz and hype there is in any presentation, the less importance and truth it contains.

I am reminded of a reference in the Hebrew scriptures where the presence of God is described as being not in the mighty, raging storm, but in the small, quiet breeze.

We don't have to worry about the truths that come to us with dazzle and glitz, because we'll get those with little effort. But let's show some active interest in those unadorned truths that take effort to achieve.

Today, enjoy any glitz that comes your way, but watch for the unadorned truths.

A Hard Question

How much is enough?

               —Bill McKibben

It seems that our national policy, one that influences all levels of society, is that any successful enterprise must always get bigger. Isn't there a time when we arrive at enough? It's time we all asked ourselves the question that naturalist Bill McKibben asks: "How much is enough?"

So many organizations, from corporations to churches, speak of themselves in terms of being growth-based. In other words, they are always getting bigger, thereby presumably increasing whatever it is they want to accomplish. It's the way our system works: Our economic and cultural systems are based on growth. So to attack that idea is understandably unpopular and risky.

But not to attack it is setting a course to disaster. Somehow we need to wake up. Saying these things out loud, as does Bill McKibben, is like rousing a sleeping giant who is blissfully dreaming behind a Do Not Disturb sign. Don't expect a warm response.

The sides are drawn: On one side are the growth-is-always-good ideologues, those that believe that things will work out as they always have, the content and satisfied. On the other side are the environmentalists, the ecologists, the poets and visionaries, the back-to-the-Earth tree-huggers, and the alarmists.

My problem is that I want a both/and solution to this problem. And while I have no doubt where I stand ideologically—I vote with the Sierra Club recommendations in hand—I don't always live that way.

I suspect I have a lot of company. What I want is not only to say, "That's enough!" but to believe it so deeply that I put it into practice, or better, I make it part of my practice.

Look for ways today to say, "That's enough."

Work and Play

All work and no play make Jack and Jill dull kids.
  —traditional saying (adapted)

Perhaps this adage grew out of the nineteenth-century Industrial Revolution in England, when many children knew little of play and too much of work. Think of Oliver Twist.

Our own age has nothing to crow about when it comes to balancing work and play—though we're talking about adults now. Ask anyone who works with families—physicians, counselors, nurses, lawyers— workaholism is alive and well, too well. Workaholism is not the same as working hard; it is compulsive, or addictive working; there is a loss of control. And it certainly isn't just Jack that's affected; Jill has long ago joined the ranks of the dull.

Everyone acknowledges the prevalence of workaholism and everyone seems to decry it, and yet we don't attain the balance we say we want. How did we get into such a sorry state?

I wish I had a definitive answer for that. Maybe the answer is very simple: Play more!

Ask yourself some questions to get you going: How do you play? With whom do you play? Do you play at all? Games? Sports? (These are not always play). Have you forgotten how? No problem: just watch children for a while. Then ask to join in.

Also, there is a simple but often overlooked fact: It is extremely difficult to achieve this balance between work and play, given the realities and demands of work and private life. It almost never happens on its own. You have to make it happen in accordance with your values and your priorities, and with purpose and planning. Otherwise, most of the time work wins.

Play today. Play more all the time. Do you need a plan to make it happen for you?

What Do I Need?

Less is more.

—Robert Browning

Recently I was in a computer store to buy ink cartridges for my printer. While I was waiting to pay, an enthusiastic clerk was unpacking a brand-new computer for display and was telling me how wonderful this top-of-the-line computer was. Its speed and capacity were state of the art. It left competition in the dust and would give me incredible advantages.

I was hooked. I wanted it. No, I *needed* it, and began to figure out how I could get it.

Later I was telling a friend about the new computer I was going to buy. She said, "Why do you need a new computer?" I answered her question by listing some of the computer's statistics and capacities. "Yes," she said, "but why do you need all that?"

"Why do I need it? Well, I . . . ."

What I really needed was her question. I was asleep, put into a trance by the compelling glitz of something shiny-new. I recognized it in the moment I was unable to answer her with any kind of honest and meaningful response. The truth was, not only did I not need the new computer, I did not even want it. Then how could I have gotten to the point of almost buying it?

It is because an overwhelming number of cultural pressures are exerted upon you and me that tell us we need things we don't need. They are powerful forces. Being awake—and also having awake friends who ask us questions—is the best defense.

Spend some moments today becoming awake to the difference between things you need and things you don't need.

eight

Finding
Peace at Work

Weariness

Our greatest weariness comes from work not done.
—Eric Hoffer

More than anything, our work represents the Mountain of Too Much, the overwhelming amount of things we have to do. Cramming more things in and cutting old stuff out are obsolete ways of coping that are no longer effective. And the Mountain of Too Much still rises up before us.

Our feeling of weariness comes not from the work that we have already done, nor even from the work that we are doing, but from the work we have left undone, or the work that is still ahead of us.

Or more specifically, what tires us most is not work, but the anticipation of work still to do. Here is a time when living in the present moment is vital. The past is gone, the future is just a concept and a projection of our minds. All you have is now. It's all you need.

So, there you are, facing the Mountain of Too Much in the form of a desk piled high with so much work that it is difficult to estimate how long you'll need to finish it. It's a moment for a Stillpoint at the foot of the Mountain:

Take a deep breath. Another. *I will just be still for a moment.*

Close your eyes. *What is past is past, I let it go. Who knows what lies ahead? Now I will do as much as I can, as well as I can.*

Invoke something spiritually meaningful. *I receive abundant grace and have my spiritual practice to support me.*

Talk assuredly to yourself. *This is my life right now. I have a Mountain of Too Much in front of me. But this burden too will pass.*

Count your blessings. *I am grateful that I have work, that it's a beautiful day. . . .* And *then* start climbing the mountain—a little more confident, a little less weary.

Today, notice how you deal with work yet to be done.

Calendars

There can't be a crisis next week. My schedule is already full.

—Henry Kissinger

I have often remarked that losing my appointment book would lead me to an enforced Stopping. I would have no other choice because I wouldn't know what I had planned. As soon as it goes into the calendar, it seems to go out of my mind.

We are often, like Henry Kissinger, run by our schedules, slaves to what we have to do, to what we have been asked to do, to what we think we should do, and, yes, to what we want to do. All this scheduled doing can get us into trouble. We can lose perspective.

What if you were to apply the following categories to your weekly schedule to find out the percentage of time you spend in each: spiritual practice, leisure, work, reading, time with spouse or partner and family, Stopping time, exercise and sports, child care, housework and cooking, errands, and time with friends. Would the real percentages match your desired percentages?

Here's another exercise. Prioritize the above categories, numbering them from the most important (first) to the least important (last). Again, do the actual priorities match what you want? What are the categories that, in real life, tend to be ignored? Do you find, like most of us, they are the items that you enjoy and that are good for you, like leisure, reading, Stopping time, time with family and friends? Again if you're like most of us, you probably don't actually schedule these things.

Start now. Get out your appointment calendar and schedule those items you tend to skip. If we're going to be slaves to our schedules, we may as well have schedules we love!

Today, spend some quiet time with your calendar.

Learning to Stop

I'm struck by how seldom company builders consider the question of what to stop doing.

—Jim Collins

Jim Collins wrote an article in *Inc.* magazine titled "Pulling the Plug." His idea is that if you "want to make room for all those new projects" then you better "stop one thing you're doing right now."

Because it will be disastrous if you don't. There's only so much time, and only so much can fit in it.

It seems so hard for us to end things: to close a business, to stop volunteering, to close up shop, to shut down a church, to end a program, to discontinue a tradition, to quit a service. Our usual decision is not to end one thing and begin another, but to keep doing the one and add on the other. It gets us into big trouble.

In his article, Collins gives a personal example. "In my left hand *War and Peace;* in my right, the TV clicker." TV usually won out, he explains, so he clarified his priority and "jettisoned the TV." His "reading productivity soared."

Ask yourself at the beginning of any new activity or program, as you start any new assignment or responsibility: Do I need to stop doing something in order to do this? And more important, is there anything I can in fact stop doing in order to do this? If so, what?

Will you begin a half-hour exercise program? What half-hour activity will you end? Want to spend a couple of hours each week reading? Are there two hours available? Where can you pull the plug?

Notice today if there is something you want to stop in your life.

Love It or Hate It

My father taught me to work, but not to love it. I never did like to work and I don't deny it. I'd rather read, tell stories, crack jokes, talk, laugh—anything but work.

—Abraham Lincoln

Honest Abe tells it like it is, I would guess, for many of us. Love work or hate it, we have to do it.

But so many of us live for the weekends. We face Blue Monday. We say T.G.I.F. We see work as a necessary evil. It's very easy to be negative when it comes to work, but that negativity can wear us down and we accumulate a lot of depressing energy over the years. Before we know it, it's become our dominant attitude toward life.

So even though there are some things we cannot change, and even though work, or aspects of it, could well remain something we don't particularly like, and even though we might not easily change work....

Is it possible for me to put emphasis on the positive and ask myself how to find affirmative aspects of work to focus on?

Are there people with whom I work that I like, whom I look forward to being with?

Can I bring what I enjoy to my work? (Lincoln would—and did—bring storytelling and joke- cracking to his work.)

What part of my work is most fulfilling to me? When do I feel that I am of the most value or performing a task I enjoy?

Who benefits from my work, even remotely? How can I keep them in mind as I go about my job? Where do I find joy in my work?

Whether the answers come quickly and easily, or slowly and with difficulty, continue to seek them. Life is too short and wonderful to allow work to ruin it. Or maybe you agree with Ronald Reagan: "They say hard work never hurt anybody, but I figure why take the chance."

Today find some new joy in your work.

Preparing

Get there early. Visualize what you want to happen.
Breathe. Have fun.

—Canadian speaker

I wish I could remember the name of the personable, Canadian speaker who said these words, because I would thank him. I heard him on a taped interview and made a special point to remember his self-counsel as he prepares for a speech. It is a wonderful formula for preparing for anything. It has helped me in many moments as I have anticipated a seminar presentation, an interview, or just an ordinary conversation.

Get there early. This gives you time to become acquainted with whatever space you will be in. It gives you time to adjust to any surprises and last-minute changes and to meet some people who will be involved in whatever you are doing. It gives you time to notice.

Visualize what you want to happen. Before you get there, days ahead of time, rehearse in your mind what you *want* to happen, how the event will ideally unfold. In your mind's eye, play it out and see it developing exactly the way you want. This is the part that may surprise you. Visualization or mental rehearsing can have a powerful influence on what actually happens.

Breathe. Conscious breathing is fundamental to any awareness of being present in the moment. It focuses the mind and spirit. Holding back the breath, or breathing shallowly, tightens the body, closes the soul, and limits the mind.

Have fun. If you enjoy yourself as you speak to me, as you share a meal with me, or as you attend a meeting with me, then I probably will follow your lead. And we'll both do what we are doing better, be more awake, and ultimately be more successful.

Do you need to prepare yourself for something this week? Get there early, visualize, breathe, and have fun.

Stress at Work

It's not the something you do. It's that you do something.

—adage

This is, without a doubt, the most important concept to understand in order to deal with stress. If you do not get this idea, you're likely to become discouraged.

The only thing that's important in managing stress, especially immediate stress—like too much to do at work—is that you do something in response to the stress. What you do is much less important than that you do something. So often we worry and fret about knowing exactly the right relaxation exercise or breathing technique, thinking, If only I could find exactly the right way to respond to this stressful situation I would be okay.

When all the time the only necessary thing is to take charge and do something, almost anything will do just fine. And, to continue the paradox, often the best thing to do is to find a way to do nothing.

Are you facing a huge pile of work on Monday morning and feeling overwhelmed?

Pause a moment, breathe, and say to yourself, I have enough time to do everything I need to do today. Or stand and go to the window for a moment, breathe deeply, and recall the joy in your life. Or stretch your arms and invoke your spiritual practice. Or visit the rest room for a moment of quiet reflection alone. Or gain perspective on this overwhelming moment by closing your eyes to recall your past—where you've come from—and then project the future—your goals and hopes.

Do these, or whatever you decide to do at the moment—as often as you need to throughout the day.

Today, in stressful moments, do something.

Breathing In, Breathing Out

Bringing awareness to our breathing, we remind ourselves that we are here now.

—Jon Kabat-Zinn

B reathing is home. It's where you can go when you're not sure what you need, when you don't know what else to do, when you can't seem to quiet that chatter in your head. It's home because it's where you can go any time at all and it always feels like you're welcome, you belong.

You go home to breathing by focusing your attention on it. For example, you've just hung up the phone after a stressful and tension-filled conversation with Harry. You're packing your briefcase before leaving work and want to do a Stillpoint at the end of your workday. Here is what might be going through your mind:

This has been a really awful day. So just quiet down, take a deep breath, and turn your focus inward. . . . That damn Harry would have to call and demand my report a week early. It totally screws up my plans to get out the . . . wait a minute, I'm supposed to be doing a Stillpoint.

Take a deep breath again and…what does he expect me to do in so short a time? I bet he wouldn't put up with that kind of abuse, I bet…wait a minute, I'm supposed to be doing a Stillpoint.

Take another breath, and ease into a calmness.…I hope he loses his job, that would serve him right, he's always making things difficult, and not only for me, but for…WAIT A MINUTE!

Okay. I'm too wound up. Now I'll just pay attention to my breathing. Breathe in, breathe out…breathe in, breathe out…breathe in, breathe out…in…out…in…out…keep my focus just on my breathing…in and out.

At any time, in any place, when you need to be calm, when you're upset, when you're distracted and can't seem to do what you want to do, focus on your breathing.

Go home every day, several times a day, by just consciously breathing.

Home from Work

———————————

Look, it's silly for you to come home from work miserable every day. Why don't you just stay there?

—woman greeting husband at the door,
in a *New Yorker* cartoon

The old days of "Hi Honey, I'm home!" are, if not long gone, going quickly, surviving mostly in *Leave It to Beaver* reruns. The *New Yorker* cartoonist captures the homecoming in a funny and not-so-funny way.

In the new paradigm, everyone comes home at the end of the day, unless, of course, you're telecommuting or work in your home.

In all of today's possible scenarios, there is an important moment to pay attention to: the time when you end work and transition to the remainder of the day—whether that's going to the gym, shopping for dinner, coming home, or all of those. Mark the end of work, and the beginning of your other life, with a Stillpoint. For many, this is the major Stillpoint of the day. Consider:

You leave your work responsibilities at work, making a point not to bring them home with you.

You change your clothes, at least symbolically, to indicate that you are moving from one part of life to another.

Often the rules change too. At home, you must operate more out of your heart, rather than out of your head.

After work, you move into a world that is often already in progress and has its moods, its history, and its needs. You need time to catch up.

If you work at home, look for signs and symbols that indicate your change from work life to home life.

Bring to mind the usual way you make the transition from your work life to your personal life. Is it a successful transition? What kind of Stillpoint would make it better?

Today, begin—or develop—your end-of-the-workday Stillpoint.

A Leaf

—✦——————————————————————————✦—

I lean and loaf at my ease observing a spear of summer grass.

—Walt Whitman

That was the worst meeting I have ever attended. I drove too fast out of the parking lot and headed into traffic. *That pointless meeting went an hour longer than it should have.* I'm hot and annoyed and want to be home.

I turned into the park near my home, quickly parked the car, walked to a nearby bench, sat down, closed my eyes, took a couple of deep breaths, and sat still.

I sense the movement of something close to my face. It's quiet and leafy. I'm not alarmed; the movement is gentle. I keep my eyes closed and slowly turn my head; and now I know it is a leaf. But there is no tree close by, is there? Is someone here and teasing me? I sense no one near.

I open my eyes and indeed see a leaf. It is spring-green and delicate, and the farthest reach of that big oak some twenty paces away. How unusual that a leaf is all the way over here, hanging in mid-air where it is not expected and getting my attention.

It is translucent, vibrant, yellow-green. It has delicate veins that reach back to the trunk and nourish it. It flutters in the breeze. It is newborn and will die in a season and will do both with joy and color.... It loves rain and sun and...is one of many and...it is exactly and completely what it must be and....

"Observing a spear of summer grass," or a leaf, or indeed any expression of nature can calm you, bring you back to yourself, away from the tensions of the day.

"How was the meeting?" a colleague calls to ask soon after I return home. "The meeting?" I ask. "What meeting?... Oh, that meeting!"

Today, encounter a tree, notice a rock or a leaf, or observe a spear of summer grass.

nine

Embracing Life

Delight Deficiency Disorder

———————————————————————————————

*It's not likely that our patients are ever going to be able
to enjoy their lives any more than we enjoy our own.*
—Paul Pearsall

Paul Pearsall, a therapist and popular speaker, has identified a serious and rampant spiritual problem: Delight Deficiency Disorder. He says:

"We're being held captive by health terrorism, viewing ourselves as more fragile and vulnerable than research shows we really are. We've forgotten that pleasure is an adaptive sense, too." The symptoms of the Delight Deficiency Disorder "include the 'cynical set' of chronic feelings of anger, irritability, aggression, and impatience.... When you're not getting delight in your daily diet, your body begins to starve for its spiritual nutrients."

Pearsall is talking not just about therapists, but also parents, teachers, and all of us. We can become so serious and controlling.

The antidotes? Lighten up! Enjoy life as much as it allows you to! Laugh a lot every day! Don't take everything so seriously and realize that in most ways, we have no control at all. Says Pearsall, "If you don't find a balance between pressure and pleasure, your epitaph is going to read 'Got everything done, died anyway.'"

I am reminded of a meal shared with friends a few days ago. After it, I remarked that they were a couple who really enjoyed life: They loved the food, clearly enjoyed each other, and seemed to be delighted to be with all of us. Their lives are not extraordinary, except maybe that they clearly do not suffer from DDD.

They are an example for me. They embody Pearsall's words quoted above, which imply that your living a life of delight will encourage me to do the same.

What antidotes to Delight Deficiency Disorder will you begin today?

Folly

The highest form of bliss is living with a certain degree of folly.

—Erasmus

Now there's a welcome bit of wisdom, I'd say. Desiderius Erasmus, a Dutch scholar and philosopher, lived at the end of the Middle Ages and the beginning of the Renaissance, and he seems to have achieved a balance that takes some good from both.

Note the meaning of his words: Bliss denotes ecstasy, spiritual joy; folly is defined as a lack of good sense, an action having a ruinous outcome. We don't generally associate one with the other. He says the highest joy admits a degree of foolishness. I find this an attractive idea; do you? Let's apply this sixteenth-century insight to our third-millennial lives. What might it look like?

Imagine a stockbroker in his mid-thirties with a dark suit and conservative tie. He works in a high-rise office in a big city and commutes to work. Now see him in full leather, on his Harley-Davidson, screaming along the coast highway headed from California to Canada.

Or imagine a housewife with two kids in school. She lives in a suburb, is a member of the P.T.A., is petite and polite. Now see her as a belly dancer, both as student and performer.

These are real people who have noticed an attraction to something that many would call folly, who have the courage of their convictions. And it makes them happy.

So this advice of Erasmus has got me thinking: Where's my degree of folly that leads to bliss? What is that element in my life that answers to no rational accounting, that many would call foolish or silly, and that would bring disdainful looks from the more staid and less blissful?

Has it got you thinking too?

Name your folly. Or pick one!

Missing Our Lives

When we lack the proper time for the simple pleasures of life...then we have missed the purpose of life.

–Ed Hays

One of the strongest and lasting images of my life is the vision of myself as an old man, waking up early one morning, and realizing—in the cold, gray dawn—that I had "missed" my life. In my vision, I would know in that moment of truth that I had not been awake, had not been aware of the pleasures I truly wanted, and had been afraid to risk. It would be a moment of overwhelming sadness.

My vision is fearsome, but my fear gradually lessens as I take time, throughout my days and years, to reconnect to myself. So I try to move into my vision and spend time with it and ask it what it wants from me, what it has to give me.

I am not the only one with this fear of missing something important. Jack Kornfield makes a similar point: "As you walk and eat and travel, be where you are. Otherwise you will miss most of your life."

Ronald Dahl is a physician and parent. He wrote in a recent issue of *Newsweek* about the pace of life and his concern about its implication for our well-being. "I sensed the fear that I may miss chapters [in his children's] childhood amid my hectic, overfilled life."

He too, it seems, has a fearful vision: waking up one morning and realizing that his children are gone, and worse, he doesn't know them.

Consider what "missing your life" might mean for you. What will you most deeply regret having not been, or accomplished? How can you begin to live so that you will be present to what is most important to you?

Today be with the question, What must I not miss?

First, Stop...

Many search for happiness as we look for a hat we wear on our heads.

—Nikolaus Lenau

Have you ever had the experience, perhaps to the delight of others, that Lenau describes: looking for something while all the time it's with you?

Looking for your hat or watch or glasses, when all the time they're on you, is, well, embarrassing. Looking for happiness in the same way can be tragic.

The poet reminds us, once again, of what we have heard so many times, and equally often have forgotten: Fulfillment—or happiness—does not await us in some faraway land of promise, or even over the next rise. It is very close to us, right here, even now.

But how tempting the faraway places are! How alluring are unattainable lands! How full of intrigue and promise! How full of adventure and, yes, fulfillment, happiness, and peace. Until we get there. Then we notice the mosquitoes, the climate, and all the differences that we are not used to, and that tire us. And we begin to think of home.

So what does it take to notice something that is very near, that I am looking for, that I don't see? What does it take to find the hat on our head?

First, we stop looking. Then we sit down a moment. Enjoy the sights in front of our eyes. Stretch a bit and scratch our head.... Ah, there it is!

What does it take to find our watch? First, we stop looking. Then sit down a moment. Stretch and breathe and notice the world around us. We wonder what time it is.... Oh, there it is!

What does it take for any of us to find happiness? First we must stop looking and sit down a moment....

Looking for something today? First stop looking. Then sit down....

Conscious of Our Treasures

*We can only be said to be alive in those moments when
our hearts are conscious of our treasures.*

—Thornton Wilder

It started out like the retreat from hell. I had been
anticipating my week-long, silent retreat with great
expectations. This was intended to be an experience
of doing nothing, just being quiet and reflective. The
point of this kind of retreat is to be alone, silent, and
undistracted. It began to fall apart right away.

The director who was assigned to me—a guide to
check in with briefly every day—was sick. The weather
was horrible, unseasonably rainy and cold. I arrived
half ill, with flu symptoms. My room was dark and
cold. Still, I was determined to make the best of it.

Then I received word that a close friend was in a
hospital near the retreat house and was undergoing
emergency surgery. That did it. I felt my long-antic-
ipated time of peace and quiet was totally sabotaged.
How could I not go to visit my friend every day,
especially since he had no friends or family in the
area?

Contrary to those early unfavorable signs, things turned out well: My friend recovered quickly, the sun came out, I felt great, and I still had two days of retreat left. Then it happened, what Thornton Wilder refers to in his words above.

Walking quietly on the grounds, with nothing particular on my mind, I was quite suddenly overcome with—gratitude. In Wilder's words, for a moment my heart became conscious of what I treasured. I felt nothing but grateful for what life had to offer.

Let us—all of us—continue to seek "those moments."

"Those moments": Today, recall them, and be open to them.

Time Runs Out

Many people die with their music still in them....
—Oliver Wendell Holmes

What an enormously sad thing to say about someone: His imprisoned music was buried with him, never to be expressed; her lovely sonatas will never bring joy and intimacy to a human heart. We'll never know what they might have been.

One of the goals of everyday serenity is to help us give expression—full-throated, out-loud, vibrant expression—to whatever music dwells in our souls; be it the music of accounting, the harmony of teaching, the notes of repairing, the symphonies of poetry, the melodies of marketing, the tunes of programming, the rhapsodies of selling, and on and on through the whole gamut of human states, activities, and gifts.

Oliver Wendell Holmes continues his thought by asking a question about his statement: "Why is this so?" And he answers it: People die with their music still in them "too often...because they are always getting ready to live. Before they know it, time runs out."

Can you, like me, remember occasions when what you were thinking sounded something like: I just have to wait 'til such-and-such happens, then I'll be able to. . . . That's getting ready to live, not living. Living is what's going on without you while you're waiting for such-and-such to happen.

And ultimately, unfailingly, absolutely—time runs out.

Time is always running out. The young can't really know it; the aged know it too well.

So for those of us in the young, old, or middle times: Play your music! However it comes out. It's yours. It's wonderful. Who knows who might begin to dance? And it won't be buried with you!

Find a song never sung before. Sing it today!

Laughing

Laughter is the shortest distance between two people.
–Victor Borge

W hatever you do, don't lose your sense of humor." Those were the words my father said to me when, after schooling, I was leaving home to take on the world. I remember two things about the moment: First, I scarcely noticed that he said it, recalling it only after several years. Then I wondered why, of all the words he might have said, he said those.

I now know—and have long known—why he said those words. He knew I needed to hear them. Life has a way of getting very serious.

But humor is attached to every aspect of human life. When you tickle the funny bone, you massage the soul. As G. K. Chesterton said, "When once you have got hold of a vulgar joke, you may be certain that you have got hold of a subtle and spiritual idea."

But mostly, humor connects us one to another. Echoing Victor Borge, Eva Hoffman speaks of an experience we've all had when meeting someone new: "There's nothing like a gleam of humor to reassure you that a fellow human being is ticking inside a strange face."

There's no one so off-putting as she who takes herself too seriously. There's no one so attractive as he who easily laughs, especially at himself, as well as at your jokes.

Speaking of jokes, did you hear the one about the two Irishmen who went to heaven and discovered that it was well beyond their expectations. "What a grand place this truly is!" said Pat. "Indeed," said Mike, "and to think if it weren't for all the exercise and health food, we could have been here years ago!"

Says Nicholas Chamfort, French writer and wit, "The day on which one has not laughed is surely the most wasted."

Look for times of laughter today.

Taking a Chance

Chance is the pseudonym of God when he did not want to sign.

—Théophile Gautier

So often good things happen as a result of taking a chance on a losing bet. It's a form of paradox: What seems to be the wise course isn't necessarily; the expected outcome is replaced by a surprise.

Years ago, while I was working at a social service agency, a young man of about twenty-five approached me with a typical hard-luck story. He was AWOL from the army. He was broke and wanted to borrow money for bus fare to return to his army base in Kansas where he planned to turn himself in and try to work things out.

Oh, sure. Likely story. "If you give him money, you're more naive than I thought," was a supervisor's direct way of stating his opinion. Others agreed with him. So did I. So I said no to the soldier.

But he was determined, and in the end, his determination prevailed. I loaned him the money.

Of course, I didn't tell anyone at the agency and about an hour after I gave him the money and he quickly disappeared, I had profound remorse. Live and learn, I said to myself.

Live and learn indeed. I got the money back—with five dollars interest!—in the mail about two months later. With it was a simple note that said: Thank you for trusting me.

But I didn't trust him, I thought. No one trusted him. But I must have trusted him, at least for a moment, and it was at that moment I acted. Of course most of the time, you don't get the money back.

So? The human heart *wants* to trust and sometimes it works out. Once in a while, take a chance—the occasional surprise is worth the failures.

Today, look around for a chance to take a chance.

Consistency

Do I contradict myself?
Very well then I contradict myself,
(I am large, I contain multitudes).

—Walt Whitman

Whitman certainly agrees with his contemporary admirer, Ralph Waldo Emerson, who calls "a foolish consistency the hobgoblin of little minds. . . ." and with Oscar Wilde, with whom he had much in common: "Consistency is the last refuge of the unimaginative."

But I find myself at times almost slavishly tied to being consistent, to being stable (read "boring"), to being trustworthy ("dull"), to being reliable ("predictable"), to being loyal ("unthinking"). Stable, trustworthy, reliable, and loyal are wonderful characteristics, of course—when they are not masquerading simply as, yes, consistency.

Teenagers know about inconsistency; it's their territory.

Sally was sixteen and passionately enamored of anything Brazilian: Rio, men, soccer, men, gemstones, men, and so on. She would learn Portuguese, marry a wonderful, rich Brazilian man, and be incredibly happy. She was adamant; this would be her life. She was also driving her parents crazy. They were concerned that her obsession was unhealthy and decided the best response was to stop fighting and join her. Her seventeenth-birthday surprise was Brazilian music and videos. They even suggested planning a family trip to Rio.

"Rio?" she screamed in tears. "Who would be caught dead there? I'm moving to Paris as soon as I graduate! *Merci! Au revoir!*"

Sometimes, don't you wish that you could give yourself permission to express that kind of wild inconsistency? I think we often feel it; like Whitman, we are large and contain multitudes.

Today be creatively inconsistent, and enjoy it.

Keeping Perspective

The reason angels can fly is that they take themselves so lightly.

—G. K. Chesterton

Often at our large family gatherings there were several guests present who were not relatives but friends of family members. This particular Thanksgiving gathering was no different.

One of the guests was a woman who, I believe, was an antique dealer from New York. She was about sixty years old, with a regal—or was it haughty?—bearing and an intriguing accent.

As the party was nearing its end, she came up to my father, took him aside, and said in a clipped voice which barely concealed her slight:"I vant to tell you that vun of your relatifs has just calt me a baloney-nose!"

Recognizing one of my uncle's favorite epithets, my father responded with laughter and the advice, "Oh, don't think anything about it. That's Uncle Stevie. He calls everyone a baloney-nose, especially if he likes you."

Her response was to be insulted for the second time.

Sometimes it is difficult to tell an insult from a harmless remark or a lighthearted tease. I can recall responses I've made which I wish, in retrospect, I could change from a frown and a grimace to a smile and a laugh.

Losing perspective is one of the effects of being busy and stressed—we take ourselves too seriously because life has us by the throat. Quiet times alone can help you know, for example, when a comment is harmless and when it's not, when it's a joke and when it's hurtful.

Taking ourselves lightly is joining the angels.

Look for an occasion to fly today.

ten

Paying Attention

Magnificent World

The moment one gives close attention to anything, even a blade of grass, it becomes a mysterious, awesome, indescribably magnificent world in itself.

—Henry Miller

I s there any greater gift than the gift of close attention? Can you recall how you felt on an occasion when the person with whom you were engaged was totally focused on you, eager to know your thoughts, and genuinely interested?

I wonder if you have in such moments the same feeling that I have? When you pay close attention to me, I feel respected. And thus respected, I will do my utmost to make what I am saying or what I am doing the very best it can be. Why? Because I know that you are really listening and taking me seriously.

Your attention calls forth my best efforts.

Close attention is one of the finest gifts we can give our children. It is to them as water and warm sun to a blooming flower. It calls forth their best.

But novelist Henry Miller is taking this a step further. He speaks of paying close attention to a blade of grass, and says that it too will respond by putting forth its best and become "awesome" and "magnificent."

Why not? When you pay attention to me you will see in me what might have, without your attention, remained hidden, even from me. So with a blade of grass: When you pay it attention, you will see what has been there all along, but is now, with the gift of your attention, revealed.

Pay close attention and open an indescribably magnificent world.

Decide now to whom or to what you will pay close attention today.

The Attentive Heart

When your heart is attentive, your entire being enters
your prayer without your having to force it.
—Rebbe Nachman

The key words in the wise man's teaching are "without your having to force it." What are the manifestations of an attentive heart?

When your heart is attentive you notice what is not there more than what is there, the subtleties more than the obvious.

You notice the quick, wan smile of a friend as she says that everything is fine.

You notice that your colleague is absent from a meeting he always looks forward to.

You notice that when I greeted you this morning I had an expression of unusual joy on my face.

You are aware that your work partner arrives later than usual. You wonder why.

When your heart is attentive you notice the presence of the divine everywhere and all the time, in a handshake, or a smile.

The attentive heart is in love with life and all its expressions and, for the most part, doesn't miss those expressions, no matter how subtle or indirect.

Having an attentive heart is just another name for prayer.

Your heart is attentive, but yearns to be more so. The moments and hours you spend in peaceful quietude are to the heart like moisture and sun to a tree. They transform your heart from the dryness of distraction to the vibrant life of seeing what's truly there, that is, to attention.

It happens on its own, "without your having to force it."

Today be conscious of what your heart notices.

Live for Today

She was saving it for a special occasion. Well, I guess this is the occasion.

—quoted by Anne Wells

One of the fundamental purposes of Stopping is to help us live in the present moment. The past is gone; the future might never be; all we really have is now. Living in the present moment also helps us not to miss what is important and to avoid what is trivial.

The words quoted above appeared in an article in the *Los Angeles Times.* The author is quoting her brother-in-law. The "it" referred to is a woman's slip, a very expensive and elegant one, that had been bought years earlier and saved for a special occasion. The next lines in the article read:

> He took the slip...and put it on the bed with the other clothes we were taking to the mortician. His hands lingered on the soft material for a moment, then he slammed the drawer shut and turned to me: "Don't ever save anything for a special occasion. Every day you're alive is a special occasion."

A time of loss—especially the death of someone we love—is a time we remember what is important and what is not. It is a time to see that so many occasions are special, like dinner tonight, or an outing this weekend, or watching your favorite TV show with someone you love, or a walk with your dog.

The challenge is to remember, day in, day out, the specialness found in the ordinariness of our lives.

Think of a special ordinary occasion (the sunset? the presence of one you care for?) and how you can celebrate it today.

A Gift from a Cat

Animals are such agreeable friends—they ask no questions, they pass no criticisms.

—George Eliot

You're walking down the street in your neighborhood and notice a small, black cat several yards ahead of you. She is looking at you.

She doesn't move as you approach. You stop, stooping down to her level, and slowly reach out a hand to her. She rubs against your hand in a friendly gesture and enjoys your scratching behind her ears. You stay there some moments.

Your blood pressure lowers.

Your breathing slows down a bit, is steady and full.

Your mind disengages from the worries and concerns of just a few moments ago.

Your facial muscles relax.

Your eyes soften.

Your voice lowers to a soft tone.

You are speaking soothing word-sounds to the cat, a mantra to yourself as well as to her.

You feel the softness of her fur, the movement of her supple skin over her neck and shoulder bones.

The vibrations of her purring soothe you.

You are quiet. You are only here. Only now.

Then she's off to other places and adventures.

And you too continue on your way to other places and adventures, but changed by a gift from a cat.

Find an animal, make contact. Today.

Talking About Weather

There are seven or eight categories of phenomenon in the whole world worth talking about, and one of them is weather.

—Annie Dillard

How did it come to be that the phrase "talking about the weather" means talking about nothing important, or nothing in particular?

You only have to imagine the magnitude and variety and power of weather to see that Annie Dillard is surely right.

We always have weather to talk about, no matter what kind. It's also a safe subject; you can have strong opinions on what it's going to do, or whether or not you like what it's doing now, and no one will think the worse of you.

But the most potent aspect of the weather is that it is a colossal force over which we have no power. We live—and sometimes die—at its will.

Its effects on human life and history are evident and immense: It has caused the winning and losing of wars, the division and unity of nations, the discovery of continents, the crossing of mighty seas, the migrations of peoples, and the way our bodies are formed, and it is a significant control system of our entire universe—just for starters.

Those are good enough reasons, surely, to talk about it. But I think I know an even better one. The weather always affects how I feel; it always influences just how I am in this particular spot on the Earth. Always.

The power of weather over us is equal to the power of water over fish. And sometimes just as hard to notice. Talking about it helps us to become more aware of its power, and thus to become aware of our state of being just now, to know just how we are feeling—always good information to have.

Several times during the day, notice the weather, its changes, and how it is affecting you.

Notice Buildings

Architecture [is] worth great attention.

—Thomas Jefferson

We are offered so many wonderful opportunities for quiet, reflective moments by noticing the buildings that are part of our lives, especially in a city. Wherever there are people, there are buildings, and they are of an endless variety of shapes, sizes, and materials.

Consider the skyscraper: soaring, majestic, defying gravity, full of so many expressions—noble and otherwise—of human life and commerce, a true symbol of our business-centered culture.

Regard the church: a place set aside, often an asylum, meant to be a safe place, a place of welcome and spiritual values, sometimes competing with the skyscraper, sometimes overshadowed by it.

Behold the shack: tumbledown, poor, and simple. Struggling to stay upright, but possibly a home to genius and virtue.

Look at your city or town hall: What can it tell you about your place on the Earth? Can you even picture it in your mind? Is it arrogant and thrust upon the world with bold architecture, or is it modest, hidden, uncomfortable with display?

Observe the museum and the library: built to last for the ages, to hold what we most appreciate and admire, to show off our talent and ingenuity, to treasure what we love for the generations.

Finally, look upon your home. It is, as author Clare Cooper Marcus reminds us, a "mirror, a reflection" of yourself. Regard it quietly, carefully.

Moments of paying attention to architecture, using Jefferson's happy phrase, are moments of remembering, hoping, and of deepening our sense of ourselves in this place.

Pick out a building today and pay attention to it.

Holy Bridges

Bridges are America's cathedrals.

–unknown

I think the meaning of this statement is that while other cultures in other times built cathedrals as the pinnacles of their cultural prowess, we build bridges. I'm not so sure this is true; we have some awesome cathedrals. But even so, our bridges are impressive as well, and the two have a few things in common.

A significant purpose of cathedrals was to provide, in the days before education was common, symbols and signs to teach faith and to remind people of those teachings. The hugeness of the building itself was the first and foremost symbol of what was most important in the community. Stained glass and graphic art were also important teaching aids.

But bridges can teach us too, if we see them with eyes open to symbols. They are the arteries that facilitate the movement of life within the community.

Like cathedrals, they are conduits that facilitate bringing two distant places together. And, also like cathedrals, they show off what we can build. They are most often beautiful; by their nature, they seem daring and bold.

I easily bring to mind two important bridges in my life: one is huge and bold and industrial-looking; the other a one-lane, muddy path over some logs.

What bridges are in your life? What can you notice about them? A quiet mind sees that bridges can not only get us from here to there, but can be symbols to enrich the meaning of life.

Learn today from your bridges: past, present, real, or symbolic.

Use Your Senses

Make the most of every sense; glory in all of the pleasures and beauty which the world reveals to you....
—Helen Keller

Glory in all of the pleasures" of the world. It's a message we don't often hear, or perhaps more accurately, we don't often hear it in a context of wholesomeness and integrity, and without guilt. Helen Keller, the American writer and lecturer, who was both blind and deaf from infancy, offers it to us in that context. "Make the most of every sense." Every day offers us feasts:

Look at shapes and colors. Trees. The sky at any time of day or night. The shape of a building. The color of a child's eyes. The picture on your wall. The reflection in your mirror. Your eyes, like an athlete's muscles, develop with training.

Listen to the world's sounds. A speeding train. Songs of birds. The tap-tap-tap of your computer's keys. Music. Your loved one's words, such as "Hi Mom, I'm home!" or "Hello Dear, how was your day?" or "I missed you so much!" To enhance what you hear, close your eyes for a moment.

Feel the world's textures. The feel of the cloth in your clothing. The handrail as you climb the stairs of a building. The erotic energy of your lover's touch. The skin is the body's largest organ. Spend a moment and notice what you feel on its entire surface at any given moment.

Taste the world's flavors. Chewing a macaroon. The taste of a postage stamp. Swallowing cold orange juice in the morning. Savoring tastes also has the advantage of slowing down your eating.

Smell the aroma of life. Passing by heliotrope or jasmine. Your perfume or aftershave. Someone else's. Walking into a very old house. A fragrance that reminds you of something long ago and far away. Especially when you want to remember something, pay attention to smell.

Make the most of every sense, today.

Observe Faces

———————————————————————————

I'm not a dictator. It's just that I have a grumpy face.
—Gen. Augusto Pinochet

At fifty everyone has the face he deserves.
—George Orwell

I think I'll never tire of looking at faces, even of grumpy dictators, and whether deserved or not. (Can you deserve a face?) As I look, I muse:

Now there's a face that shows such care and compassion. And here is another, which shows suffering nobly borne.

His carries a deep anger and irritability—it's in the way he holds his mouth—which seems to indicate an unhappy man.

This child's face is all mirth! Such an unrestrained smile and uninhibited, delighted laughter.

There's a dour quality to that lady's face. I wonder what experiences have made her so? But no! Now that she smiles and laughs, how could I think her dour?

Shyness shines out of this man's eyes. I have a hunch he would make a good friend. His wife is by far the bolder; her eyes hold power.

Deep creases in sun-darkened skin, squinty and rheumy eyes, and wisps of white hair. He has been to the mountaintop and survived. I wonder if he is a good teacher? I'd bet so.

Reflect on the faces of your life. Perhaps take out some photos of family or friends, maybe of your grandparents. Contemplate those faces and notice what you see there.

And then stand quietly before a mirror, soften the muscles of your face, look with soft eyes, and smile.

Today, notice the faces of people you encounter.

Guardian Angel

I am the bird that flutters against your window
in the morning,

and your closest friend, whom you can never know....
    —Rolf Jacobsen (Translated by Robert Bly)

One of my earliest memories is of my guardian angel. It was an encounter when I was about five. I was alone in my room on a summer's morning. The window was open. I heard my name called twice, very clearly. I asked everyone in the house and even the neighbor lady if they had called me. They all answered no. So by a process of elimination, I knew, very matter-of-factly, who it was. I was not particularly impressed; I merely had figured out who it was and went back to play.

We live in a culture fascinated by angels; we encounter their images everywhere. I believe, for the most part, we see them for what they are: expressions of the divine presence. They transcend and inhabit many religious traditions. And they seem to be very popular on television these days.

By nature elusive and prone to metamorphosis, angels invite to us an encounter only if we are still.

I am the thought that occurs to you out of nowhere, the idea that comes to you sudden and unbidden. I bring you that happy feeling and you say, "Where did that come from?" I am the stranger that helps you along your way, the friend who appears when you need me. I am a messenger from other worlds. I am your shadow. I am your best friend "whom you can never know." I look at you with longing.

I can never forget you. I know all that you were meant to be.

I am the miracle that saves you from some disaster, the hand that holds you from the fatal step.

And when you need to, I just let you go on your own.

Today watch for signs.

Snapshots

Remember what you have seen, because everything forgotten returns to the changing winds.

—from a Navajo chant

If you're like me, it almost goes without saying: Going on vacation? Take the camera. And how many pleasurable moments I enjoy looking over the snapshots from some past outing or adventure.

But taking a photograph does not mean that I will truly remember the moment, the place, and the persons the photograph captures. To truly remember, I must mindfully look, clearly see, and—most especially—deeply feel during the moments I am in their presence. Only then will I remember.

Mindfully look: This means to dwell some moments with the image before you, allowing the lines and colors and presence of the scene to make an impression on you.

Clearly see: Gaze, ponder, distinguish, compare. You might notice that the color of the marble in the building reminds you of the pink flesh of fresh salmon.

The far sides of the mountains before you in the late afternoon sun actually are purple.

Deeply feel: The cityscape in your viewfinder brings back a memory of another time and place. The five people posed in a smiling and bantering group evokes a feeling of right now—this time, this place, these people, this light—that you want to keep.

These are what you first notice and remember, what will give depth, meaning, and insight to the way ahead. Then take the photo, which becomes the timeless vehicle of the moments it captures. Otherwise we have only snapshots, and the rest is lost, "returns to the changing winds."

Next outing: First look, and see, and notice your feeling. Then, take up your camera.

Realizing Life

*Do any human beings ever realize life while they live it?—
every, every minute?*

—Emily in *Our Town*

At this point in Thornton Wilder's play, Emily is a ghost; she has just died and is allowed a brief visit back to life. The godlike stage manager gives, of course, the only real answer to her question: "No." But after a pause he adds, "The saints and poets, maybe—they do some."

I like this definition of saints and poets: they are everyone who has some capacity to realize life while they live it. That definition can include you and me, no matter who we are or how busy.

We don't have to be compared to Albert Schweitzer or have published books of poetry either. We just need, as much as we can, to realize life, now.

How do we realize life? Emily's ghost, who is allowed to return to Earth for her twelfth birthday, answers for us as she speaks to her mother who, still in human life, is—as mothers do and need to do— prattling on to her about eating slowly and keeping warm: "Oh, Mama, just look at me one moment as though you really saw me."

And then to the stage manager Emily says, "I can't. I can't go on. It goes so fast. We don't have time to look at one another. I didn't realize. So all that was going on and we never noticed."

Yes, it's all going on right now, today, this minute. Do you notice? Take Emily's advice: Look into the eyes of those you are with as though you were really seeing them, that is, attending to them as fully as you can, being aware as much as possible of all that is going on in the moment.

Join saints and poets. Today look at someone as though you were really seeing him or her.

Talking with Things

―――――――――――――――――――――――

If you love it enough, anything will talk to you.
—George Washington Carver

It is not unusual, in my practice as a family therapist, to hear someone very cautiously admit that they—only rarely, of course—talk to themselves, occasionally even out loud. Somehow, this practice has become associated with an expression of crazy behavior.

I believe it can often be a very healthy thing to do. It's a great way, for example, to cover all sides of an argument you're having with yourself. (The key, of course, is to know with whom you're talking.)

But what about not only talking to yourself but talking to things, and then having things talk to you? Have we gone over the edge here?

Can we really hear things talking to us? I would say yes and no. Take the no first: If I walk outside and ask the petunias for the time of day, please come and get me help. While the yes part of my answer is stronger, there is the qualification that Carver mentions: Things will talk to you only if you love them, and only if you have ears to hear.

What Carver, the brilliant agricultural scientist, teaches us with his words is what he must have experienced in his life. He worked with things like soybeans, sweet potatoes, and cotton and discovered hundreds of uses for them. He focused on them, he studied them, he learned all about them, he used them, tasted them, and lived with them.

He loved them. They spoke to him. They revealed to Carver the secrets they kept in their fleshy hearts.

He took time to listen to them. He was quiet enough to know he loved them, and they talked to him.

What part of this wondrous world do you love? Perhaps you already know that it talks to you. If not, listen carefully.

Today notice what things you love. Then listen.

Overlooking

"How are you today, Mom?"
"I'm fine—if you overlook a few things."

—from a conversation with my mother

The other day when I was in a local bookstore, the owner recognized me from a recent book signing and, after greeting me, said, "I want to tell you how much I appreciate your story about your mother. I've used those words many times." My blank look encouraged her to continue: "How your mother said, 'I'm fine if you overlook a few things.'" Oh, yes, I recalled mentioning that, as a passing remark.

But she recognized a significance in the words that I had missed. Her recognition became mine when she gave it back to me.

Certainly one of the greatest challenges in our relationships—in raising children, thriving with a significant other, having friends, getting along with coworkers—is to know when to notice something and, especially, when not to notice. In other words, we have to learn a scale of priority with which we choose our issues; the lesser ones can slide, the greater ones we face.

My mother's words, spoken when she was aging quickly, are an example of how she picked her issues.

And now, how often the words come to me. How many opportunities I have to "overlook a few things": my own aches and pains, failings, frustrations, moments of impatience, or another person's fumbling, forget-fulness, or other foibles.

When we are stressed and overloaded, it's easy to lose a sense of proportion. But in the quiet times of life we can remember what is important and what is not so important, what to notice—and what not to notice.

Today be aware of your choice: To notice or to overlook a few things.

eleven

Knowing
Thyself

Not Forgetting

If I forget thee, O Jerusalem, let my right hand forget its cunning. If I do not remember thee, let my tongue cleave to the roof of my mouth.

—Psalm 137: 5-6

As I recall the final years of my parents' lives, I note that they were characterized by a continually failing ability to remember. At first it was mostly short-term events and people that would not come back to them; later they lost almost all recall of the distant past, or of a few moments earlier.

It was then it struck me: how much of life is not forgetting! Not just in a nostalgic way, like recalling the summer of your twelfth year, but just keeping in mind all the information you need to operate through the day.

Imagine beginning today with amnesia. There would seem to be nothing to be, nothing meaningful to do. Life would have no purpose.

Imagine life without our ability to remember the past, to tell our history, to gather our stories. Not only would we be doomed to repeat, we would not even know we were repeating.

"Everybody needs his memories," says novelist Saul Bellow. "They keep the wolf of insignificance from the door."

Recently I visited the Holocaust Museum in Washington, D.C. Talk about the importance of remembering! This entire endeavor is built upon the word *remember*. And as we speed up, forgetting creeps in—insidious, secret, and pervasive—so we must put ever more effort into this kind of remembering.

There are so many people, so many things, so many times and events to not forget, but to remember!

How will you make today a Day of Remembering?

What People Say

———————+—————————+———————

If three people say you are an ass, put on a bridle.
—Spanish proverb

I don't think any one of us is immune from the powerful influence of our neighbors' opinions. We're just built that way. What people think of what we do, how we act, what we wear, how we smell, and the way we talk and walk—all of those attitudes affect us. Especially powerful are people's opinions of who we are.

Of course, we are always telling ourselves, rightly so, that it shouldn't make any difference what people say; we need to do exactly what is most true for us.

Of course. But if three people say I am an ass, what then? My first inclination is to say I'll wait until it gets to four or five people before I'll take it seriously. So if five people say I am an ass…? What then?

The proverb seems to say there's wisdom in what people say of me, and I should listen to it, especially if several say the same thing.

I have to agree. If several people say the same, it's probably true. At least it's true that I appear that way.

And it doesn't mean that I have to change. Perhaps, with Thoreau, I hear a different drummer. Then I must step to the music I hear, "however measured or far away." It just means that's how people see me. What people say is a mirror, a way to self-knowledge, a standard, and a measure of how I compare to public standards.

From quiet moments of contemplation and stillness will emerge your authentic response to what people say about you. For myself, I think I'll keep a bridle hanging close at hand.

Today consider what people say and your response.

Invisibility

What is essential is invisible to the eye.

—Antoine de Saint-Exupéry

I was working with a client on stress management and asked him in my routine questioning if spirituality were part of his life. "No," he answered, "not at all. In fact I don't really know what you are talking about when you ask that."

I responded with a brief and uncareful definition of spirituality, thinking that this would give him a sense of what I meant.

"But that definition can mean anything and nothing," he said. "You really aren't telling me what it is. The word *spirituality* really makes no sense to me. It's just some well-intentioned but make-believe gibberish."

I engaged the challenge because, in many ways, his response was right on. My definition was intended for one who already accepted what I was talking about, not for someone who did not.

"What is valuable to you that is invisible, not directly perceivable by any of your senses?" I asked.

In the process of answering he came to such values and meanings as "love of family" and "meaning of my faith" and "honesty" and "responsibility" and on and on. These are invisible in themselves, made visible only indirectly when they are acted out. They are beyond monetary value, ultimate, and essential. No one can be alive without them, although they certainly differ from person to person. We all have spirituality. It may or may not be part of a religious faith.

What is invisible is essential, says Saint-Exupéry, novelist, aviator, and adventurer. And what is invisible and essential becomes visible only to those with eyes to see, eyes that have been opened in quiet moments of stillness.

Take some moments today to name your invisible essentials.

Eulogy for a Wonderful Life

What a wonderful life I've had! I only wish I'd realized it sooner.

—Colette

Bittersweet words these. How much better to realize how good life is—as much as possible—all along its course. That's one of the main purposes of achieving serenity, realizing life as you live it.

Colette, the French novelist who died at eighty-one in 1954, indeed had a full and meaningful life. She was a music-hall dancer, mime, socialite, wife—she married twice—and famous writer.

Most of us, especially when we compare ourselves to those we see as rich and famous, like Colette, feel that our lives are fairly dull and unimportant. Not so, if only we could realize it now.

So here's a suggestion to help the realization. Write your eulogy, what could be said about you at your funeral. It will feel, after the first moment perhaps, far from morbid; it will bring a new realization.

When I tried this process, the first thing I felt was panic. I couldn't think of anything to write, at least anything that I considered worth writing.

With persistence, it began to flow, not great and magnificent deeds—I still don't have those—but whom I loved, who loved me; what I valued and how I expressed it; when I was there for someone in need, and when I accepted their being there for me; what I really enjoyed and what made me laugh. Now I can go on and on. So can you.

This exercise has a bonus: as you prepare "what they can say about me when I'm gone" you will simultaneously create "what they can say about me while I'm here"! Your exercise will serve not only as a eulogy, but also as a reminder of the good things in your life right now.

To realize your life, start writing your eulogy today.

The News

Ah, there's good news tonight!
–Gabriel Heatter

If you remember hearing those words on the radio, then you're, uh, . . . of a certain age. I recall hearing them as a boy listening to the evening news with my grandfather. Heatter, a popular news reporter of the day, would begin some newscasts with these words, trying to give hope during World War II, when most news was grim.

Most of the news is still grim. Or so it seems to me.

Perhaps more significant is that it's hard to get away from the news. At times, I try to take a vacation from watching the television news; it becomes a bit over-whelming to me. News dissemination is so constant and so widespread, however, that it is difficult not to get the news. And that has consequences.

We carry the news with us. We carry the crime, the violence, the wars, the suffering, and the pain. We carry more now than ever because we are bombarded by it constantly. This societal stress is relatively new to human life, and is added on to the already record-high personal stress that we each carry.

So we need to take charge, as much as possible, of how we allow the news into our lives:

A couple of times a week substitute Bach for Brokaw. You won't miss anything that you won't hear again soon.

Get in the habit of allowing a piece of news about suffering to trigger a moment of reflection for those involved. At least this is something we can do rather than just feeling powerless.

While you are watching the evening news, remember to breathe deeply, slowly.

Design your watching-the-news Stillpoint today.

Stories

The only thing that keeps us from floating off with the wind is our stories. They give us a name and put us in a place, allow us to keep on touching.

—Tom Spanbauer

Our stories keep us from floating off with the wind: It's unthinkable to not have a past, a history of all that has happened to you, not to remember what you have lived, or to recall the people of your life. How could you face tomorrow, even the next moment, without your stories? You wouldn't know how to be. You would simply lift up, lighter than air, and drift away with whatever wind happened along, finally becoming a disappearing speck, like a child's lost balloon, doomed to the void. Nothing would hold you here.

Your stories give you a name: What do people call you? How do you refer to yourself? If I know your stories I will absolutely know you, because they are only yours and your name is the only name on them. If you tell them right, they will remind me of my stories too.

Your stories put you in a place: You are here now. You have been here all your life, or you have only been here a few days. You have been in many other places, or very few. You may be somewhere else soon. But now you are only here. When you tell me your story, you will tell me where it happened and why you were there. And that place will have changed by your being there. You will hear the names of places and you will cry.

Stories allow us to keep on touching: You're always touching something. Sometimes you're touching someone else. Who is it that touches? Why are you touching this part of the Earth, this other human being? What stories bring you, whole and present, to this moment? Could you bear to lose them?

Spend quiet time remembering the stories of your life. Note them. Write them. Keep a list of them. Add to them.

Begin to gather your stories. Then tell them.

Waiting to Trust

He said that Godot was sure to come tomorrow.
—Samuel Beckett, Waiting for Godot

Waiting too long—putting things off—is not only an indication of fear; it may be an indication of denial or self-deception. Samuel Beckett's play *Waiting for Godot* is a fine example of paralyzing fear turned into a serious case of avoidance of responsibility.

A recurring dialogue between the two main characters in the play runs like this:

"Let's go."
"We can't."
"Why not?"
"We're waiting for Godot."
"If Godot comes we'll be saved."

And nothing will move them to get on with their lives; they are convinced that Godot will come. Of course, Godot never comes.

It is often easier to trust in the power, wisdom, and words of someone else than to trust ourselves.

A woman who works in an office is told by her supervisor that the bid she draws up should be bold and consciously aggressive. It's the only way to get the clients to accept it. She has firsthand experience of the clients, however, and knows that the opposite approach, conciliatory and soft-sell, will in fact work best.

It would be easier to trust her boss; he would also get the blame—theoretically. But she knows what she knows. How will she act? Will she, like the two characters in the play, keep waiting for the time when she acts on what she knows?

How would you act? During times of solitude and quiet, times with nothing to do, times to move into and out of fear, you can rediscover trust of self, and allow it to return to the position of ultimate power.

Is there an aspect of your life where you give too much power to someone else, where you are afraid to trust yourself?

Bird and Book

When the bird and the book disagree, always believe the bird.

—bird-watcher's proverb

When I was a graduate student I learned one of the tenants of the field of psychotherapy: Don't accept gifts from clients. Accepting gifts is therapeutically ill-advised. It interferes with the process of therapy.

So when, during my early years as a family therapist at a social service agency, my client—I'll call him Ben—arrived for his session one day with a gift for me—a small, framed photograph of the coast—I told him that I could not accept it.

Now in my heart, and even in my clinically trained mind, I knew this gift was nothing more than Ben's way of saying thank you. It was the kind of thing he enjoyed doing. No hidden agendas. It would really be okay to accept this. But when he went on to say that he picked it specially for me while he and his wife were visiting the Wine Country north of San

Francisco, I still said I was sorry but, no, I could not accept it. I also said something about rules for this sort of thing.

Ben left the session with his gift, and me uncomfortable with my decision to refuse it. To this moment, I regret my decision. I should have both accepted it and talked about it. But I followed the book I had read, not the bird I was looking at.

I'm not saying that the rule I learned is wrong, but that there are moments when you must trust what you see and feel right now, and not what the theory says, when you must trust the bird, not the book.

Watch for opportunities today to trust the bird you see, not the book you've read.

Fads

In 1963 the mere mention of the God concept was good for a laugh. By 1965 it was many people's most serious concern.

—Jeff Nuttall

What surprises me so much is not that I flit from one fad to another, from this hot idea to that one. No. What truly amazes me is the apparent ease with which I do it and how much company I have.

Last month I was focusing intently on the importance of a particular vitamin. This month someone asks me about it and I say, "Oh, yeah, I guess I ran out." Some intense importance!

A fad-dominated life is characterized by a distracted and vacant presence in the moment, by a never-ending string of disappointments, and by a palpable, but often inaccessible, sadness. It's like looking for fulfillment in way too many places. The new item that so excited me in anticipation now lies sadly forgotten—a betrayal—on the shelf.

In the young, this characteristic is probably a necessary stage of development. In adults, it is destructive because it keeps us from going deep—into our souls or into our projects—and limits maturity by keeping us stuck at a juvenile level. Of course, it is especially sad when we turn something momentous, like God, into a passing fad.

And let's not forget the formidable forces that drive the fads, and that benefit from them. Hot items sell. They have immediate interest. They entertain in the short run. They often fill an immediate urge. They are often difficult to resist.

Being still, for a while every day, and for a whole day every now and again, will clarify your fad-identifying vision.

Identify a practice or project you want to stay with, go deeply into, or even return to.

Jump at the Sun

Mama exhorted her children at every opportunity to "jump at the sun." We might not land on the sun, but at least we would get off the ground.

—Zora Neale Hurston

I appreciate this mother's effort to get her kids to become self-fulfilled. They are words of exuberance and hope. But jumping at the sun and barely getting off the ground are two different things.

Really, it's a wonderful statement of extremes: The goal is the sun, the flaming, all-consuming desire of pure ecstasy; the reality, a couple of inches off the Earth, for a couple of seconds.

I hope mothers still say things like that to their children. We need encouragement, especially when we are children, to become all that we can be.

I have the feeling, reading between the lines, that this mother was a woman who knew exactly what she was saying. If her words were taken literally, if you indeed were to land on the sun, you would long since have been incinerated to a mere speck of ash. But what a way to go!

Taken figuratively, the words seem to imply that the feeling of deepest passion and its achievement always involve suffering, an insight wise mothers know from lived experience. Thus her words both encourage—Jump for the highest goal you can think of!— and prepare for reality—Don't be surprised if you fall short, or if it's uncomfortably hot when you get there.

The saints and the poets know this. "Ah, but a man's reach should exceed his grasp, or what's a heaven for?" is Robert Browning's way to say it.

And many mothers and fathers know it too. "Jump at the sun!" is the way one of them said it.

Who said, "Jump at the sun!" to you? To whom can you say it?

From Velcro to Teflon

Each of us needs to withdraw from the cares which will not withdraw from us.

—Maya Angelou

I have a jacket that has Velcro fasteners at the sleeves to close the openings, as well as down the front to keep the jacket closed. When I wear the jacket open both at the sleeves and down the front—which is how I like to wear it most of the time—all of the Velcro surfaces are exposed, and my arm is always getting stuck to my chest.

To some of my cares I am like Velcro: We stick to each other. No matter how much I try to solve them or deal with them or get rid of them, they attach to me. My financial worries pop up while I'm enjoying dinner in a restaurant; or anxiety about an upcoming presentation seems to dwell right in the front of my consciousness.

Some people are like Teflon. Nothing seems to stick to them, at least not their problems. Carefree is what they seem to be, moving along with joy and equanimity. How do they do that? The poet invites us to discover the answer.

Taking a few moments each day to be quiet and reflect can transform our cares from sticky Velcro into non-stick Teflon. In Maya Angelou's words, "each of us needs to withdraw from the cares which will not withdraw from us."

How? The poet continues: By "hours of aimless wandering or spates of time sitting on park benches."

Coat your cares with Teflon. Put some aimless wandering or sitting on a park bench in your life today.

Living with Quandary

When one admires an artist it is important not to know him personally.

—Jacinto Benavente y Martínez

By their nature, quandaries often don't get resolved, but the attempt can be most beneficial.

About ten years ago I self-published a short psychological tract, on the cover of which I wanted to reproduce a drawing by a favorite artist.

After having given permission, the publishers wrote to say they were mistaken, that the copyright had reverted to the artist. I must seek permission from him. But I had already used the art. I was in a tough spot.

I decided to write the artist and tell him the whole story, apologizing for using his art without his permission, indicating that I indeed thought I had obtained permission, asking now for his retroactive consent to my use, and offering to pay whatever fee he asked.

His answer was immediate, full of anger and bitterness, and demanded payment of a fee four times the normal amount. It was a nasty communication that ignored all I had expressed.

This was from a favorite artist. I love his work. Copies of his pieces have hung on my wall. But now something had changed. What? It has been—and continues to this day to be—an interesting and revealing quandary for me.

As I spend quiet time with his work, I know that I still admire it, but I have seen an aspect of the artist that I can't like and that has possibly changed my attitude toward his work. Part of me says my attitude is unreasonable and unfair. Another part of me doesn't buy it.

As I contemplate his work, the quandary remains, but the process of consideration, the quandary itself, has been a benefit. It has pushed me into new territory, given me a bit more comfort with the unresolved.

Is there an unresolved quandary in your life?
Maybe it just needs more time.

Precious Bodies

Our body is precious. It is our vehicle for awakening.
Treat it with care.

—Jack Kornfield

No one would deny that we spend huge amounts of time, effort, and money trying to make our bodies more attractive.

I would make a suggestion for an additional effort: that we spend time seeing that the body we each have right now is already beautiful, awesome, and a wonder to behold.

But what about those twenty extra pounds, you might say, or my horrible hair, or my lack of hair, or the bags under my eyes? On and on we can go, focusing on all the things that make our bodies less than they should be.

When you take a moment to consider, you see those objections are based on a cultural projection. Many cultures, past and present, consider what we call too fat to be very appealing; what we call too thin to be provocative and attractive; what we call frumpy to be stylish. In present-day Western culture, only a narrowly defined type of human body is touted by the style-makers as attractive.

Somehow we ignore that only about one-fourth of 1 percent of people actually have that kind of body and they spend practically their whole lives keeping it that way so they can be photographed for the rest of us to feel bad about!

Crazy, right? But it takes time—quiet, reflective, contemplative time—to see the truth of this. The cultural forces telling you the opposite are strong. Today, be gentle and loving with your body.

A suggestion to remember today: My body is beautiful just the way it is.

twelve

Awakening
to Wonder

Hello, Life

I'm afraid if I stop, I'll never be able to start again.
—nursing seminar participant

I'm convinced one of the reasons we enjoy it so much once we begin to spend time alone and quiet is that it encourages us to take life on its own terms and make the best of it. We become disinclined to say "No!" to the realities of life, and instead say, "Hello, where did you come from? We've not spent much time together, so sit down awhile and let's talk."

No matter how much I might desire and work for a totally balanced, peaceful, easygoing, work-free, and carefree life, I'm just not going to get it, at least most of the time. The more I cope with life on its terms, the more it will respond to my coping.

I can still picture the nurse who spoke the words above at a stress management seminar. These were not casually mouthed words, but spoken from the heart. She was suffering from burnout. She had an earnest look on her face, an expression of her deep concern that she would not be able to get going again if she were to give in to doing nothing.

Can you identify a fear that brings the same kind of worrisome words to your lips? Spend a moment with a little exercise. How would you finish this sentence?: "I'm afraid if I stop, I'll…"

By spending a long night of quiet reflection, this busy nurse was indeed able to start again, and to keep on starting again, because during that quiet time she learned to engage her challenges ("Hello, life") rather than avoid them ("No!").

Begin a dialogue with the challenging aspects of your life today.

Covering Up

You can't get away from yourself by going to a booze-bazaar.

—Elbert Hubbard

No, you can't get away from yourself, but you can cover yourself, you can avoid whatever you don't want to face, by going to a booze-bazaar. The language of this saying from the 1920s is quaint to our ears, but its truth remains real.

And how good we are at covering! Often we don't even know we're doing it. We get into deep trouble by covering because what we cover is almost always what we need to face and resolve. Consider just a few covers:

Alcohol and drugs are perhaps the most common ones. A few drinks or pills, and the pain of loss or the agony of fear is less demanding, easier to ignore or forget.

Television covers a lot. Turn it on when you get home, turn it off when you go to bed. It's always filling in time that might otherwise bring you to... what?

Humor is also a way to cover. It's often difficult to name it because the response is that you just can't take a joke. If you know someone who always jokes about the issue, you've probably discovered a cover.

Work is certainly one of the most common ways to cover what we don't want to face. It has the "advantages" of being socially acceptable and often profitable. Covers are endless: food, religion, hobbies, self-righteousness; literally anything can be a cover.

For those who would like to be awake, dis-covering our covering is not only essential but enormously rewarding: You get yourself back.

Take quiet time today to dis-cover your ways—maybe just little ones—of covering.

Failing

This thing we call "failure" is not the falling down, but the staying down.

—Mary Pickford

Recently I received a phone call—a recorded message actually—that told me that my services were no longer needed at the place where I had a part-time job. I enjoyed the work I did there and looked forward to it. Now, quite suddenly, I had been dropped.

The administrator who called was clear and kind; I could tell he was sorry, and he said so in a gentle way. The reasons he gave were understandable; I would have come to the same conclusion, given the circumstances.

But the thought that came to me immediately—not thought really, but feeling—was, I have failed. What did I do wrong? I've been terminated, sent packing, dismissed. I've failed!

Well, yes. . . . But have I failed, really? There's a fine line here. On the one hand, the fact is they let me go. So in a sense, yes, I have failed. I would feel somehow dishonest, not allowed my truth, no matter how unwelcome, if someone tried to tell me that I didn't in some way fail. On the other hand, trying something, failing, then trying again, is the way to most good and great deeds. Trying again—that's the key.

"America's Sweetheart," Mary Pickford, the plucky film star of the 20s, tells it clearly: Failure is not falling down but *staying* down.

Thus I guess the question for me is clear: That's over, how can I try again?

Think of something you consider a failure. Can you—or did you—get up and go on? The only failure is staying down.

Giving Fear a Name

<hr/>

Whatever our crisis, whatever our sorrow, whatever our feeling, to name it is to frame it. A frame of words gives us the safety to claim our feelings as our own.

—Gabriele Rico

Years ago a client came to my counseling office telling of almost constant, fearful anxiety. A married businessman in his mid-fifties, he had felt shame and discouragement for many years, but finally decided to come to counseling. We had only two sessions.

During the first session, I asked him simply to tell me the story of his life. He more than filled the time with a condensed version of his life, hitting all the major peaks and valleys.

A week later, as we began the second session, I mentioned that I appreciated the trust he showed the previous week and I noted it must have been especially difficult to talk about the years of sexual abuse as a child. Those were the words I used.

He looked at me astonished. "Abuse? What abuse?" he asked. I related back to him his recounting of ongoing and traumatic years of childhood sexual abuse. He sat stunned. He had never thought of it as abuse.

At the end of the session I said that I would see him next week. He replied something like this: "No, that's all I need. It all makes sense to me now. I was abused, yes, I see that now. So my frustrations and feelings make sense. It's okay now. Thank you."

I tried, without success, to get him to return for some more processing. But to him, he got what he needed: Now this fear had a name.

Sometimes it's that simple. When you name something, you assume a position of power over it. You've "got it" in a new way and it no longer "has you." I hope that was the case with my client.

What fear can you give a name to? Is it the name of a person? An event? A possibility? Speak its name today.

Telling the World

The most effective step in dealing with any fear is to some way, any way, tell it to the world. If you don't do this, the fear will get stuck. It must be told!

This process can be exquisitely simple: Have you ever had the experience of feeling better, feeling relieved, because you had just gotten something off your chest and told a friend about it?

The process can be magnificent and it doesn't have to be only in words. Listen to Beethoven's *Ninth Symphony,* for example, and you are experiencing that composer's narration of his strong, brooding fears, his deep hope for joy. He narrates them in music. Or you can dance your fear, or sculpt it, or draw it, or write it, and so on. Literally anything can serve as a telling to the world.

The narration can also be entertaining. When I first read the above quote from Alfred Hitchcock, I was struck with his clear, simple statement of narrating. What he feared, he expressed to the world in scary, suspenseful films. As we experience his fears through the film (I think of the way I felt watching *Dial M for Murder* and *Rear Window*), they become less of a burden for him. By his process of narration, we participate in his fears.

But we not only share these fears; they also serve us. Artists, like the musical composer and film director, have expressed to us, have entrusted us with, their feelings. The resultant music and films are wonderfully beneficial: The symphony lifts our spirits, the film delights and entertains us. Narrating puts you in touch with the world and the world in touch with you.

Try to find a way to express something you fear to some part—big or small—of the world today.

Reframing Grief

In grief we face a sacred moment, one permeated with
fear, overflowing with pain, steeped in difficulty.

—Molly Fumia

Often what prevents us from creating quiet space in our lives, what keeps us from the essential joy of doing nothing, is the presence of grief. It is a formidable presence and, understandably, our first response is to avoid it.

Grief is always about loss, the anguish and pain we feel when we lose someone or something precious to us. And it regularly happens to all of us. It is one of our most familiar common grounds. No one is immune.

I believe one of the first signs that we are ready to face grief is our willingness to stop, to be quiet, and to be with ourselves.

This is a sign of the sacredness that author Molly Fumia speaks about. Grief is sacred because it can, perhaps more than anything, bring us into contact with ourselves. (In her brilliant and powerful book

Honor Thy Children, Fumia relates the story of parents' loss of all three of their children, and of their journey to a noble response.)

So consider: What am I sad about today? Then just allow the feeling of loss, the grief, to be there a moment.

Even though grief involves fear and pain, and even though we initially run from such things, Fumia continues, the "sacredness is in the sound of our returning footsteps." Having grieved, we return to life, to ourselves, with a new compassion, a new understanding, and even a new joy.

> *Today spend some time feeling one of your losses, and listen for the sound of (or the promise of) your returning footsteps.*

Mad or Sick

I don't express anger, I get a tumor instead.
—Woody Allen

"You've got to get in touch with your anger" is the kind of thing many people think therapists always say to their clients. We therapists, so the belief goes, always want people to get angry and to express it—vehemently.

Not true—at least not any more. Recent research has shown that getting the feeling out in a concentrated way—punching a pillow or throwing rocks as an expression of anger—is not only ineffective but countereffective.

A better understanding comes from emphasizing the importance of truly feeling any emotion you happen to have—anger, joy, sadness—and then expressing it in an effective, moral, and legal way.

That might not be the direct expression of the feeling, but a healthy sublimation of it: expressing anger at your child's death caused by a drunk driver by forming an organization to educate and control drunk driving; expressing your frustration with graft by researching and writing on it.

The point is that we have only two choices—It's either get in touch with it by acknowledging and expressing it, or risk burying it, which means it will get in touch with you by becoming a tumor in your gut, or any one of many other illnesses.

Not that all illnesses are the result of unexpressed feelings, but buried feelings can and do transform themselves into disease.

It seems to me that this process also has to do with healing. You can't *cure* a feeling, that is, just make it go away, but I believe you can *heal* it. You can find a way to express it to the world.

Today, look for occasions to creatively express a feeling.

An Unwanted Grace

I'm glad that damned horse fell on me. It made me lie still in one place and look at you.

—Andre Dubus

The words are from a Dubus short story, "The Colonel's Wife." Col. Robert Townsend, a tough, retired marine who has seen a lot of action, speaks them. His horse has fallen on him and terribly crushed both his legs, possibly beyond repair.

The words, said to his wife, Lydia, were a long time in coming, a long time of pain, anger, and frustration. But he could finally say them because—I'm interpreting his sentiments—of what the accident made him learn about himself, about her and their life together, and about what is truly important and what is not.

His long, forced time-out was unwanted, perhaps like one you or someone close to you has experienced from an illness or accident. Such an event keeps you still, unable to go about life as usual; it is a forced quietude.

It's not the optimal way to be still and do nothing, but it is often the only way some of us can wake up and remember what we want and need to know. For some of us, life has to knock us about a bit before we get the idea. The important thing is not to miss the opportunity, even if it comes in a deplorable form.

The story ends on an upbeat note. The colonel got what he needed from his long time of doing nothing. Dubus ends his story with these words about Col. Townsend: "He wanted to know only what had happened and *what was happening now,* to see that: brilliant as the sky, hot as the sun, bright as Lydia's eyes." (Italics mine.)

A question to keep in mind today: What is really happening now?

Sing, Dolly! Sing!

She retreated to the mountain cabin she was raised in and settled down for an extended stay.
—*USA Today* on Dolly Parton

Public performers and artists are always under pressure not only to perform, but also to be innovative and entertaining. Sometimes the well dries up and they search for a way to find new life and energy.

What Dolly Parton did was what I call a Grinding Halt.

"I went there to figure out what I wanted to do now that I'm at a turning point," she says about her withdrawal to her mountain retreat.

She's fifty-two, a good age for a long Stopping; they often come to us in mid-life.

The *USA Today* article points out that Dolly had not had a hit in years, hadn't starred in any recent movies, and that the TV series she was working on never made it off the drawing board. So she withdrew to her mountain cabin for a long, quiet time.

But now, she says, "I've never been more excited or felt more creative in my life. I feel like I'm just starting the second part of my life and it's going to be even better than the first half."

For Parton, her Grinding Halt was also creative time. The article indicates that she had no intention of writing songs, she just went away to figure out what to do, but "that's when the songs started coming," she says. In her three-month Grinding Halt—a long one by any standard—she wrote thirty-seven songs.

Sing, Dolly! Sing!

Are you in mid-life? Consider a Grinding Halt. Or at least a Stopover of three hours, or three days.

Where Am I?

—————————————+—————————————

If we could first know where we are and whither we are tending, we could better judge what to do and how to do it.
—Abraham Lincoln

Where are you and where are you going? If we know the answers to these questions, Lincoln reminds us in his direct, unadorned style, we can make much better life decisions.

I would add: We must not only attempt to know the answers, but we make every effort to remember them, and keep them up-to-date.

Some years ago, I was at a seminar presented by the well-known author Sam Keen. He gave a wonderful example of Lincoln's truth. He was speaking of marriage, and, if memory serves, of his own experience.

Too many of us, he taught, make the decision to choose a life partner before we begin to answer Lincoln's questions for ourselves. The result is that, because we are not clear about where we are, nor about where we want to go, we are in poor position to pick a lifelong companion for the journey; if we get the right one, it's more a matter of luck than wisdom.

One of the best times for a long period of doing nothing, a Grinding Halt, is before a major decision, like choosing a life partner, having a child, changing your work, reentering the work world, retiring from work, or moving across the country.

It's during a long time of peace and quiet that you have a chance to begin the process of forming answers to Lincoln's questions.

Are there major decisions ahead for you?
Schedule a Grinding Halt now.

thirteen

Connecting
with Others

Just Being

Nothing happens next. This is it.

—Gahan Wilson

In a *New Yorker* cartoon, Gahan Wilson shows two Buddhist monks seated next to each other, quiet, still, meditating. One is very old and experienced in the ways of meditation. The other is young and has a perplexed look on his face. It's evident that he has just asked his more experienced mentor a question. The old monk's answer to the question is: "Nothing happens next. This is it."

I like the cartoon because I have often identified with the young monk. "What happens next? Isn't the idea that something is supposed to happen? When nothing happens, isn't that a waste of time?"

I also like it because it has a clear and important message for the way we live in these millennial times. Like the young monk, we need the wisdom of people who have spent time being quiet, listening to the heart, learning the questions that only silence can reveal, absorbing the life-giving silence, and being as aware as possible of this moment.

We need old wisdom. The wisdom of crones and shamans, of wise priests and rabbis, of discerning souls who have spent time on the mountaintop.

The young monk's question is based on a firmly established assumption in our Western minds: It's what *happens* that's important. And, of course, often that's true. But what happens is also the part that is easy for us to understand. The part we don't understand is the old monk's answer, "Nothing *happens* next." There is no event, but there is something. There is, in fact, everything.

The cartoon implies that when the old monk is long gone, the young monk will be there to take his place and thus the wisdom will continue.

Today, as you move through your day,
remember that this is it.

Let's Talk

We're in such a hurry most of the time, we never get much of a chance to talk.

—Robert M. Pirsig

Whatever happened to conversation, to the "calm, quiet interchange of sentiments" that Samuel Johnson attributes to good conversations? Or even to the "hell-fire and sparks" he names as characteristic of others?

We seem to manage quick greetings and little chats. We just don't have time for real conversation, for getting into a topic and staying with it, exchanging thoughts, opinions, and feelings about it. What is more human? What is more noble? What is more important?

One way to get off the treadmill is to take the opportunities for real conversation that crop up every day—take the time to visit a while over the backyard fence with the neighbor, to spend a couple of hours talking with an elderly aunt, and stay at the dinner table a bit longer for good conversation with family and friends. Who cares if the kids skip a bath or you miss a TV show?

By spending time to talk with those we care about, we are both the givers and the beneficiaries of the gift of presence, and we won't have to worry about, in Pirsig's words in *Zen and the Art of Motorcycle Maintenance,* "a kind of day-to-day shallowness, a monotony that leaves a person wondering years later where all the time went and sorry that it's all gone."

We will have been present enough to engage in conversation.

Today give a gift to yourself and someone else: Extend quick greeting into a real conversation.

The Inner Connection

Intimacy requires courage because risk is inescapable. We cannot know at the outset how the relationship will affect us.

—Rollo May

There is a most wonderful quality that results from the time we spend alone and recollected. The comfort we feel with our own inner selves will be recognized by others who are also accustomed to going within, and we won't miss the subtle invitations to intimacy and connectedness.

I remember a moment when this inner connection with another person happened for me. I was going through a significant life transition and I had just spent a long period of time alone, a month-long Grinding Halt. Soon after, I attended a large family gathering where I met for the first time the wife of one of my cousins. The moment our eyes met, I knew that she was someone with an awareness of her inner life, and an open welcome to others who would connect with her, including me.

But I felt very vulnerable and I was not ready to take the risk of opening myself up to her. So I ran, quite literally I'm a bit embarrassed to say, to the other end of the room and started a much safer conversation. I knew, from the inner connection, that she would know everything about me in about three minutes of conversation, and I wasn't ready.

Something in her and something in me connected—the inner connection—and communicated without words.

In the meantime, happily, I have been able to tell the story to the same woman, now a friend as well as a cousin.

The more time you spend in quiet recollection, the more you will notice others who do the same, and the more you will take the risk to connect with them.

Be open today to recognize an inner connection with others who also spend time with the genuine within.

A Good Model

Children have more need of models than critics.
—Joseph Joubert

Recently I was reading about the endangered grizzly bears on the coast of British Colombia. The authors emphasized how the cubs were keen observers of their mothers' skills in searching for and consuming food. What the cubs learned by the mothers' modeling was a matter of life and death; without that knowledge the cubs probably would not survive.

Our observations of bears can be so clear and accurate. With us, well, it is just a lot easier not to notice. But the same principle applies.

How can we believe that when we live life like a rat race, our children somehow will not? That as we mindlessly acquire and consume, our children will somehow know moderation and meaning in their relationship to things? When we speak with prejudice, meanness, bigotry, and hate, how can we act surprised when our children act out our words?

If I regularly cheat on little things—like not returning the extra change I receive at the counter, or pocketing found money without trying to find its owner—I am teaching that behavior to children.

Here's an example of a young person who gets this idea pretty well. A recent magazine article on parenting told of a fourteen-year-old boy who was asked to give a toast during the forty-fifth birthday celebration for his father, a successful physician. The son's toast was three words: "Dad, do less!"

"But I'm doing it all for my kids!" That's the usual excuse for our overwork, and it's probably true. But it's not the modeling by which they will, as surely as the sunrise, learn how to live their lives.

Today, consider if kids—yours or others'—would say to you, "Do less!"

Making Boundaries

Sometimes, when one person is missing, the whole world seems depopulated.

—Alphonse de Lamartine

Where are people in your life? Are people in your life the way you want them to be? Clear, strong emotional boundaries allow us to enjoy our relationships with others in ways that are healthy for all.

Boundaries are important because otherwise we make some painful mistakes: You spend a lot of time doing things for other people when you really don't want to, and then you resent it; you think someone is a close friend but he would be surprised to hear it; you wake up one morning to realize that you really don't know the person in bed beside you.

In order to live a peaceful and balanced life, we need healthy boundaries, limits that allow us to say no, to avoid overcommitting and having to respond to everyone's needs. Healthy boundaries are flexible and you're in charge of them.

Watch for signs of weak or unhealthy boundaries:

Telling intimate information about oneself to inappropriate people or strangers

Assuming deep friendship when one is only an acquaintance

Inviting yourself to places where you are not invited or expected

Inability to say no, even when you think it's wrong to say yes

Feeling responsible to fix everyone's suffering

Inability to detect the "rules" that apply to professional and personal relationships

A symbol for confused boundaries: clenching your hands together. A symbol of too rigid boundaries: stretching your hands wide apart. A symbol of healthy boundaries: clapping your hands.

Today pick a challenging relationship in your life and consider it in terms of healthy boundaries.

Allowing

The first faults are theirs that commit them, the second theirs that permit them.

—eighteenth-century English proverb

Years ago, I recall watching the following interaction on a daytime talk show: The guests, seated in a row, were four or five men and women who had been divorced for a number of years. After brief interviews with each of them, the host escorted onto the set each of their former spouses, seated them opposite the guests—all of them had by now remarried—and proceeded to mediate a dialogue among them all.

The interactions were fairly predictable until one of the women asked her former husband this question: "I've never been able to understand this: Why did you treat me so badly?"

Without a pause, without even a blink of the eye, he answered, "Because you let me."

All these years later I still recall how his words impressed me, surprised me really, and taught me a lesson. I think his answer was brutally honest.

I find it impossible to defend his reason or to admire his actions, and there's no way to know if his former wife really "let" him. But the fact is there are people who will hurt you if you let them. To put it in extreme, but clear, language: sadists find masochists.

The same man said something like this to his ex-wife: "I was wondering when you would tell me to stop, but you never did, you just got more and more hurt."

Even though forgiveness is a spiritual goal, "to forgive," as Jack Kornfield says, "does not mean we will allow injustice again." Saying, "No. This can't go on. I won't allow it. Just stop it" is often the first step in stopping an injustice.

Is there a place where you need to say no?

Crying

It opens the lungs, washes the countenance, exercises the eyes, and softens down the temper, so cry away.
–Charles Dickens

I t's easy to imagine these words tumbling out of the officious and self-impressed Mr. Bumble who simply dismisses a child's sobbing, determined to remain unmoved by the tears of the poor orphan, Oliver Twist. His words do, however, express the benefits of crying, which, in a culture that is more likely to bolster the opposite view, are not to be put off lightly.

Crying has a bad rap for adults and it's time to change that. So I'll add a few comments of my own to Mr. Bumble's.

First, crying does not necessarily indicate sadness, and it rarely indicates weakness. But that's as far as many of us go with crying: sadness and weakness. How did we come to such a wrong-headed conclusion?

Crying is not an emotion in itself, but a comprehensive expression of all deeply felt emotion. Crying can express any feeling: tears of laughter or weeping of sorrow, sobs of delight or wailing of grief, tears of excitement or crying for joy.

But oh, how we resist! Somehow we have the fear-based assumption that when someone cries, we must do something to make him or her stop. Our fear will flee, however, when we get the idea that we don't have to do anything to stop another's tears, we have only to respond appropriately to the feeling the tears express. It's the deeply felt emotion that likely makes us uncomfortable, not the crying itself.

Crying is, ultimately, profoundly human. Poet Heinrich Heine captures that fact nicely: "Whatever tears one sheds, in the end one always blows one's nose."

When you feel like crying, cry. When you're with someone who cries, let them.

Enemies?

Pay attention to your enemies, for they are the first to discover your mistakes.

—Antisthenes

Part of what Antisthenes, the fourth-century Greek philosopher, states here isn't anything I didn't learn long ago, namely, the person who dislikes me the most is the one who knows my weaknesses. The other part, the first part, about paying attention, well, I'm still working on that.

There was this guy. I don't think I have ever disliked anyone so much before or since. I'll spare you the details, except to say he was mean-spirited and had an uncanny accuracy in zeroing in on your most vulnerable spot. And he never hesitated to do so.

Well—and here's the hard part about all this—he was almost always right. I mean his criticism was basically accurate. The mistake I made or the fault he named was real. I was served up the truth in a nasty and ill-willed manner.

Did I dislike him for being mean? Or was it that he was right and I didn't want anyone to notice it? Or both?

In any event, he was still right. That's the philosopher's "pay attention" part, the hardest part, which can come to you only as you sit quietly and try to be open. The more we can see our enemies as teachers, the more serenity and peace of mind we'll have in their presence.

Look to people—maybe not true enemies, but people who oppose you, who have a different set of assumptions from you, who don't see things the way you do, or even who don't like you. They may have something valuable. They may be able to help you see your mistakes, the areas in which you need to grow, or the hidden areas of your personality.

You don't have to like them. That guy I was talking about? I still don't like him, wherever he is.

Watch for opportunities today to learn from enemies.

In the Meantime...

For what human ill does not dawn seem to be an alleviation.

—Thornton Wilder

Therapists know this, so do parents. Time heals. You'll feel better in the morning. The weight and ache of grief will ease with the passage of time. Rest works its blessings.

But therapists and parents also know that, in the meantime, when you are in pain or sorrow, it is a great help to have someone who will be with you right now. This someone is a "friend who shows love in times of trouble," Epicurus reminds us from the third century.

When hurt and pain are the only things I feel, "in the meantime" is right now; it's in this moment when the words "You'll feel better in the morning" don't help much. These in-the-meantimes are a frequent occurrence for most of us, for there always seems to be more than enough pain and suffering to go around.

Thus we have many opportunities both to need the presence of a friend, and to provide it.

When you go through a period of sorrow or pain, remember it is important to ask a friend, "Will you just be here with me?"

Take a moment to think about the people you love; is there one you need to ask, "Do you want me to stay with you for a while?"

Look for an in-the-meantime when you can just be with someone, or might ask someone just to be with you.

Say It Now

There is more of unpermitted love
In most men's reticence than most men think.
—Edwin Arlington Robinson

The death of someone close to us, or especially a brush with our own death, can bring us face to face with our desire to say things to people that we often put off because they are difficult to say. Things like "I love you," or "Thank you," or "You have helped me so much."

But then time passes, the urgency of our determination wanes, and we continue to postpone saying what we feel. Until the next dire event.

Keeping this determination alive and active seems a valuable goal of one's spiritual practice.

Deep sadness and profound regret resonate in words like these: "I never told her how much I appreciated what she did for me, and how important she was in my life" or "I missed the chance to tell him he was one of the people in my life that I really loved, and now he's gone."

American poet Edwin Arlington Robinson sees this as "unpermitted love" and says that it is more often manifested in "reticence" than in actual expression. It's a sad truth.

Spend a moment and bring to mind those people toward whom you feel love, gratitude, or appreciation: family members, friends near and far, current and gone by, perhaps a teacher, an aunt or uncle, a neighbor, a pastor or religious guide, a childhood friend, or maybe someone you don't know well, but who was there at just the moment you needed them. Think of them. Name them.

Now say it. To those that still live, tell them what you're feeling. Don't wait until a death brings you deeper regret. I think you'll love the feeling you have when you do it; I think they will love it too.

Say it today. Write the letter, make the phone call, have the conversation.

Alice

Learn to be quiet enough to hear the sound of the genuine within yourself so that you can hear it in others.
—Marian Wright Edelman

I have a friend, Alice. She is someone whom people immediately trust. Strangers as well as friends tell her confidences and know that she is respectful and trustworthy. She is not trained in any of the helping professions and she does not in any way propose that people give her these confidences. It just happens. People say to her, "You're so easy to talk to" or "You're such a good listener."

As I observe my friend Alice, I realize something. She has a stillness, a quietude about her. One might even—mistakenly, I believe—confuse her aura as sadness. It's more a sense that she has faced some of the more difficult moments of life and has come out the better for it, has come out with grace.

Alice has been able to look into her genuine self and find peace, and that fact is apparent in subtle but strong ways to those who encounter her. I believe what people see in her is her recognition of something important in them and that she is not afraid of it. That recognition is an invitation to come in, to be accepted as you are. It's an invitation home.

So spending time in stillness and solitude is a benefit to you, yes, but it is also a gift to others. You become available in a new and welcoming way to those you encounter. And it won't be because you try so hard, but simply because, if you've been there, people will recognize it and respond.

Today be aware that your quiet times will soon become gifts.

I Know What You Mean

Blade Extremely Sharp! Keep Out of Children.
—warning notice

I had a good chuckle when I read these words on a small knife I keep in my desk drawer. The product was obviously made and labeled in a non-English-speaking country. The manufacturer knew what he wanted to say, but he said something else. He meant, "Keep this sharp blade away from children." Sometimes *out of* and *away from* mean the same thing, as in, "She is out of/away from the office right now." And sometimes they don't. You just have to know.

If I were speaking to the manufacturer, I would say to him, "I know what you mean." But even in so obvious a situation, I would be hesitant with the words, "I know what you mean."

That's because I can still hear the voice of a woman from years ago. She was in deep grief over the loss of her child, a teenager killed in an accident. She had expressed profound pain and loss to which I responded with something like, "I know what you mean."

"How could you possibly know?" she said to me. "You have never lost a child."

If I could magically go back to that moment and have a second chance at my response, I would not say those words. And her words have been a valuable gift.

From that moment to this, I try to be cautious when I am tempted to say that I know what someone means. I try to pause and think, Do I really know? It's the pause—the still, reflective moment—that allows the recollection, the contemplation, the truth of the moment to open.

Those words—I know what you mean—can be a very sharp knife indeed, and should be kept out of children, and adults. Know what I mean?

Before you say "I know what you mean" try to remember to pause.

fourteen

Giving Back to the World

The Loop of Life

If you bring forth what is within you, what you bring forth will save you. If you do not bring forth what is within you, what you do not bring forth will destroy you.

—Jesus, Gospel of Thomas

The Gospel of Thomas is a manuscript that dates from the times of the four Gospels of the New Testament, but was only discovered in a cave in the Egyptian desert in 1945. Called a Gnostic Gospel, it contains some sayings of Jesus that the other, official, Gospels do not; such as the one above.

These words speak so earnestly, directly, and succinctly to the needs of our current era, it's tempting to think there was something providential in the timing of their discovery.

If what we bring forth from within us will save us, then what we bring forth must be wonderful, marvelous to behold. It must mean that we need to look within to find our truth, not out there somewhere.

The power of these words is what I notice first. They are stark and clear: There is no room to fool yourself. You either get what's in you out, or it will destroy you.

What Jesus is talking about in these words is the first and most urgently important gesture in the loop of life: What is within you is expressed to the world (it is, literally, the way you live your life) and the world receives it (however it might, with applause or disdain) and thus returns it to you. You receive it back, now changed, and process it further, and again express it to the world, forming the limitless loop of life, of communication—really, of love.

For the process to work, you need the necessary first step: time, quietude, and peace to notice and appreciate what is within.

This week, notice what is within as the first step in the loop of life.

Practice

To know the way and not practice is to be a soup ladle in the pot and not taste the flavor of the soup.

—Jack Kornfield

Practice is used here not in the sense of rehearsing, as a student might practice the piano, but in the sense of the Greek *praxis,* meaning practical human conduct, especially ethical conduct. The day-to-day way that belief is lived out is one's spiritual practice.

Practice is, as one might expect, practical. It gives you a way, a systematic set of many kinds of things to do, which express a set of convictions or beliefs.

With or without a specific religion, to attain a sense of serenity, a specific practice is vital. It concretizes and makes present what could otherwise remain only theory. Jack Kornfield says it more poetically: To have beliefs and no practice is to be the ladle and not taste the soup.

How would you finish this sentence: "I put into practice what I believe in the following ways...."

Identify your practice in a concrete way: this reading, that meditation, this act of virtue, that ritual or music, and so forth.

For many, I believe, practice is a combination of a specific spiritual tradition and one's own inclinations.

For him who has a practice, the times of trial and pain are faced with serenity and a spiritual power structure that is in place and ready. He is the faithful one.

For her who has a truly integrated practice, it is almost impossible to distinguish her practice from the serenity of her life; they are the same. She is the holy one.

*Call to mind your practice, or resolve to
define it.*

Right Here

+————————————————————————————+

Anywhere is the center of the world.
—Black Elk

"Then I was standing on the highest mountain of them all, and round about beneath me was the whole hoop of the world," says Black Elk, medicine man of the Oglala Sioux. "And while I stood there I saw more than I can tell and I understood more than I saw. And I saw," he continues, "that the sacred hoop of my people was one of the many hoops that made one circle, wide as daylight and as starlight, and in the center grew one mighty flowering tree to shelter all the children of one mother and one father. And I saw that it was holy."

And then, after indicating the specific place of his extraordinary vision—and so much in the spirit of First Nations people—he brings us right down to Earth: "But anywhere is the center of the world."

Anywhere. Especially right here, right now. Right where you are now is the center of the world. That's not because you are the most important person in the world, not because the world revolves around you, but because you are as important as any person in the world, and the world that you experience does revolve around you.

The way each of us normally experiences the world is as a center, or a point at which all comes into consciousness.

The challenge is to see the whole hoop of the world from where we are at the moment. Too often what we see is a pitiable imitation, blinded as we are by limited expectations, small hopes, and unimaginative desires.

The whole hoop of the world will include our unique hoop, as one of many that fit into the world's plan. When we see that, we know the peace that comes from being in the right place at the right time.

Today be right here. And from right here, look out to see the whole hoop of the world and your place in it.

Saying What You Mean

+––+

Some guy hit my fender the other day, and I said unto him, "Be fruitful, and multiply." But not in those words.
—Woody Allen

One of my personal goals for the past several years has been to accurately represent externally to the world what is actually going on internally: to say what I am thinking, to behave as I believe, to live the maxim, What you see is what you get. I'm still working on it. But I find it's not as easy and straightforward as it seems.

Sometimes people don't really want the truth: "So tell me, dear, how do you like my new outfit?"

Sometimes it's a question of simply being civil, like Woody Allen's comment. Many folks don't want to hear exactly what he said to the guy.

At times, when I believe a question is inappropriate, as when I answer the phone and someone immediately asks, "Who is this?" I bristle and won't say. Or when a telemarketer asks, "How are you this evening, sir?"

Courtesy, convention, and our own personal quirks keep us from saying the exact truth some of the time, and often rightly so. It gets more difficult with more important questions:

Someone says to you, "I wouldn't be caught dead with a member of that group, would you?" Do you agree, giving tacit agreement to the prejudicial comment? Or do you challenge it and cause unpleasantness?

A friend stops you on the street and asks, "Say, why aren't you coming to our meetings any more?" Do you answer truthfully that they are boring and useless, or just that things have gotten a little busy recently?

Each resolution to these challenges, whether momentous or trivial, is born out of the contemplative times of our lives, and reveals their effects.

Today, notice when you say what you mean, and when you don't.

Noticing What's Not There

Don't play what's there, play what's not there.
—Miles Davis

To live a harmonious life, we need to heed Miles Davis' words—to learn to pay attention to what is *not* there, as well as to what is; to notice what someone does not say, what example the salesperson does not use, who is absent from the meeting, or what is not included in the artist's painting. So often what is not said is the primary motivation behind what is said.

Davis cuts to the quick of the concept with his pithy encouragement to a young musician: "Play what's not there!" The statement presumes that the student can already play what is there.

I envision the response of my ten-year-old self had I been confronted with this directive from my piano teacher. It would have made no sense to me, and given me another reason to resist her influence (a resistance which, unhappily, was successful).

So how do you play what's not there?

First, of course, you have to notice what's not there; no easy task for the Western mind, which is more at home with what is there. Ask yourself, in the words of a currently popular question, What's wrong with this picture? That might help you notice.

Then you've got to put what's not there, there. I think it's the risky business of putting yourself there. Can anyone tell someone else how to do this? It depends on so much: your courage, your imagination, your will, and finding your own voice, for example. But remember something important about this process: It's great fun.

One thing for sure: When you are playing what's not there, you are soaring with the angels. And people know it when they hear your music.

Look for an opportunity today to notice what's not there.

Connecting

Connection is not something you do. It's a profound awareness of how you actually live your life.

—Paul Pearsall

Understanding this statement pushes us beyond what is often considered politically correct. But to miss its meaning causes much profound unhappiness.

Pearsall explains that certain behaviors and attitudes disconnect us from the world and from other people and we end up isolated and miserable.

Do you litter the environment? You're disconnecting from the Earth. Are you patient with a new saleswoman? You're connecting to the people around you. Are you divorced? You broke a connection. Are you marrying? You're making one. Do you pray or do your spiritual practice? You're connecting to your soul. Are you rude and self-centered? You disconnect yourself from your world.

This might seem judgmental. However, not to make these distinctions clearly, not to make these choices intentionally, and especially not to acknowledge our inferior choices readily lead only to confusion, frustration, and resentment.

This is nothing new, of course; it's the practice of virtue and the building of community. But the context of connecting seems to be important to emphasize in our age of anxiety, where loneliness is confused with aloneness and painful isolation is common.

We can know the condition of our connectedness only within the context of quiet hours of peace and of reverie. Then in our active periods we enjoy the fruit of those times of peace; their results are available to us, and tilt us in the direction we most want to go.

Notice how you connect or disconnect today through what you do.

Walking Your Talk

It's no use walking anywhere to preach unless our walking is our preaching.

—St. Francis of Assisi

Even at that time, several years ago, the speaker I was about to hear was well-known and respected; today he is even more famous. I anticipated learning a lot at this seminar. I had a deep interest in his topic, which was the relationship between stress and spirituality.

In fact, I did enjoy the seminar, and perhaps I learned more than I expected to. And yet....

Well, what happened is that the seminar room was right next to a large kitchen where they were busy all day preparing food. It was very noisy, and at given moments so noisy that the speaker had to stop his presentation and wait.

He tried several times to tell the kitchen staff to stop making noise, but it soon became clear that it was not possible to eliminate the noise and keep cooking. He was not happy about it, and it showed.

On this particular day at least, he was not able to handle this unavoidable stress with much grace. You could see him tightening up and getting angry every time there was noise. We all picked up his annoyance, either feeling it also or wishing he would seize the moment and give us an example of what he was talking to us about. But today, his walking was preaching louder than his preaching.

Any of us can relate to this speaker's plight. There are times we are just not up to the walking, and the preaching just keeps going on. Serenity will be ours every day when we are aware when we are not walking our talk, and take our own steps to get back on track.

Recall where you will be walking today, and
how you want it to be.

Happy Discovery

...like corn in the night.

–Henry David Thoreau

It is most gratifying for me to observe someone who is discovering the reality of the words: You don't have to do anything for something very important to happen.

In this happy discovery, there is a joy, a freedom, a feeling that there really is no pressure, no anxiety about performance, no test at the end, no accountability to authority whether I used the time wisely, no worry about what comes next, no important lessons to learn or heavy thoughts to ponder.

When we take time out of our hectic days to stop and remember ourselves, there is only now. And now. And now....

Then how does the Stopping work? Borrowing Thoreau's words, we grow "like corn in the night." It happens on its own.

As the corn has been planted and watered and fed, so have you. Now just let it all be there together, and what needs to happen will happen. Trying to *do* something while Stopping just messes it up.

What can you do to corn in the night to help it grow?

Leave it alone.

Find a few moments today to grow like corn in the night. Then leave it alone.

National Stopping Day

It's a good time for the nation to go on retreat, preferably a silent one.

−Michael J. Farrell

No, there isn't a National Stopping Day, but I think it's a good idea.

Michael Farrell, editor of a national weekly, thinks it should be extended to a retreat, a silent one.

His editorial appeared some weeks after the Clinton-Lewinsky affair hit the headlines. He was hard, but not only on Clinton. "No one handles the truth more loosely than the failed hero Clinton—except for the others."

You don't have to look far these days to hear how badly eroded is our trust of public figures—all of them. Accusation of wrongdoing and denial of wrongdoing both have the ring of silliness. It's impossible to tell where the truth is, where justice is.

Farrell suggests a silent retreat for all of us. I'd settle for a yearly National Stopping Day. Just imagine:

One day of the year during which no one would work. Everyone would say only what's necessary and do nothing in general but be silent and relax.

And for performers of essential services there'd be an alternative Stopping Day; the rest of us would spell them.

Everyone would be quiet and listen. The preachers. The politicians. The judges. The lawyers. The journalists. There'd be nothing on television and radio. No newspapers. No mail delivered. Only necessary phone calls. The World Wide Web would be still.

All over the country we could look at the sky, take a walk, watch the rain, listen to nature, sit quietly, look into one anothers' eyes, say a few good words, walk the dog, eat quietly, observe the passage of time.

Just imagine how we would all feel the day after! I've no doubt we'd all demand that it become a monthly event.

How would you "not do" anything if there were a National Stopping Day? Don't worry about the rest of us, just go and not do it.

Acknowledgements

I want to express my sincere thanks and appreciation:

To my brother Ewald Kundtz, Jr. for his continuing help and encouragement, and especially for his persistence.

To Brian Ganley for coming up with just the right story.

To Bob Stenberg for his on-going support and enthusiasm for my writing projects.

To Claudia Schaab, formerly of Conari Press, for improving the text and giving it structure.

To Mary Jane Ryan, executive editor at Conari, for just the right balance of pressure and encouragement; and to all the great people at Conari.

And finally, thanks again to my clients, to whom I dedicate this work.

About the Author

DAVID J. KUNDTZ, author, speaker, and licensed psychotherapist, is also director of Inside Track Seminars, which offers seminars on spiritually based stress management and emotional health for the helping professions.

He has earned graduate degrees in both psychology and theology and his doctoral degree, a doctor of the science of theology (S.T.D.), is in the field of pastoral psychology.

His previous books are *Men and Feelings* and *Stopping: How to Be Still When You Have to Keep Going*. He lives in Kensington, California and Vancouver, British Columbia.

Dr. Kundtz welcomes your communication, especially as you make discoveries in achieving a quiet mind and in your practice of Stopping. Both Conari Press and the author are genuinely interested in knowing your experiences. Let us hear from you.

Send e-mail to: dk@stopping.com
Fax: (510) 559-9193
Write: David J. Kundtz, c/o Conari Press
An imprint of Red Wheel/Weiser, LLC
500 Third Street, Suite 230
San Francisco, CA 94107
www.redwheelweiser.com

Visit the Stopping Web Site at:
www.stopping.com

To Our Readers

CONARI PRESS publishes books on topics ranging from spirituality, personal growth, and relationships to women's issues, parenting, and social issues. Our mission is to publish quality books that will make a difference in people's lives—how we feel about ourselves and how we relate to one another. We value integrity, compassion, and receptivity, both in the books we publish and in the way we do business.

Our readers are our most important resource, and we value your input, suggestions, and ideas about what you would like to see published. Please feel free to contact us, to request our latest book catalog, or to be added to our mailing list.

Conari Press
An imprint of Red Wheel/Weiser, LLC
500 Third Street, Suite 230
San Francisco, CA 94107
www.redwheelweiser.com